AF291321

Alex Head
ZK/U Press, Berlin

Third Edition
Editor: Anna Kostreva
Layout: Philipp Koller
Additional research & conceptualisation: Anna Kostreva
Illustrations of paper collage and plants by the author

Printer: Janet 45, Plovdiv, Bulgaria
Fonts: Deviancy, Suisse Works, Suisse International
Cover image: *Garden of Ronald*, in memory of the late Ronald
Harper, 1925-2015

First edition of 150 - May 2016
Second edition of 500 - September 2016
Third edition of 800 - June 2018

Published by ZK/U PRESS, 2016

ZK/U (Zentrum für Kunst und Urbanistik)
Siemensstraße 27, D-10551 Berlin
publish@zku-berlin.org

ISBN: 978-3-945659-09-0

About the author
Alex Head is an artist interested in creating non-hierarchical networks of artists, researchers and citizens.
His research is often translated into broadcast radio
programmes. He has worked with the Centre of Art and
Urbanistics (ZK/U) on a project-by-project basis since its
inception during the Wasteland Twinning Network Forum,
2012. He was born in London, 1983, and currently works
in the UK and Berlin, Germany. Head is co-founder of the
Wasteland Twinning Network. In 2017 he launched
sub_ɬxəɬ radio, an itinerant platform for discussion and
sonic knowledge production based at ZK/U and 199 Radio
London.

To
Oliver,
Amelie
&
Kobe

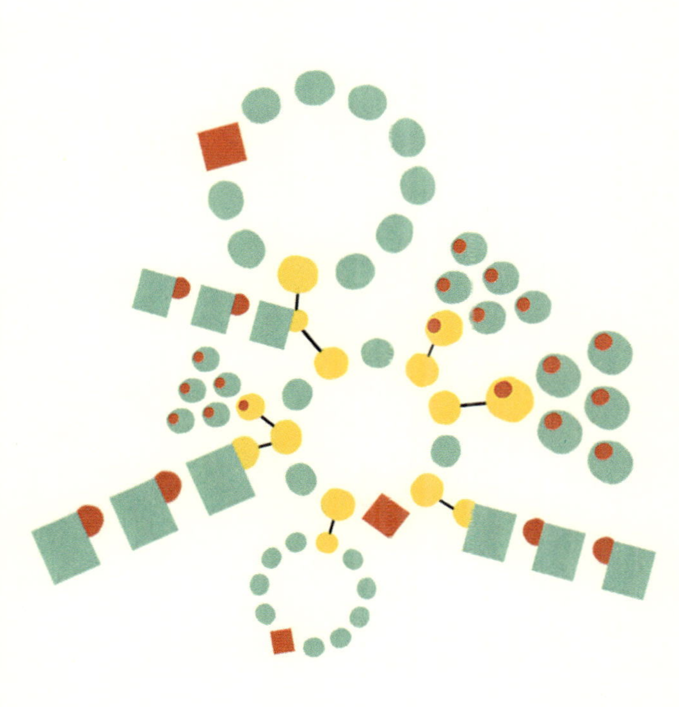

Deviancy as a Model: Exploring *Basic Thermodynamics and Language*

Imagine the outrageously tiny size of an atom. Focus on the size of this microscopic particle in relation to your own human body. Now scale up to the size of the planets, galaxies and to the solar system as a whole. The weight of your body exists between these vastly different scales.

This paper is not about thermodynamics, negative feedback or refrigerators. Neither have I written a book about geology, black holes or migration, yet each of these material systems operating at greatly different scales offer insights into the slippery topic of deviancy.

The most important goal for me has been to delve into these complex systems and extract the aspects I think help to analyse deviancy.

This is a work of material philosophical theory that is not satisfied with pure abstraction or the incestuous jargon of disciplines. In each of its diverse arguments, I have worked to harness and communicate my ideas in specialist as well as non-specialist language.

So what is deviancy?
What forms does it take historically and what,
as it were, does it do?

When I began asking this question it soon became apparent that no clear set of answers exist. As I hope this work will demonstrate, part of the reason why the label of deviancy can be so dangerous is its very ambiguity. I have chosen to explore art, madness and magic because each of these subjects involves a potential violation of what it means to be socially or scientifically 'normal'. By exploring these exciting subjects through different models, each offering new perspectives, I aim to create a large, coherent picture of how the world works in relation to deviancy. I have tried to build my arguments around models of different scales and physical states.

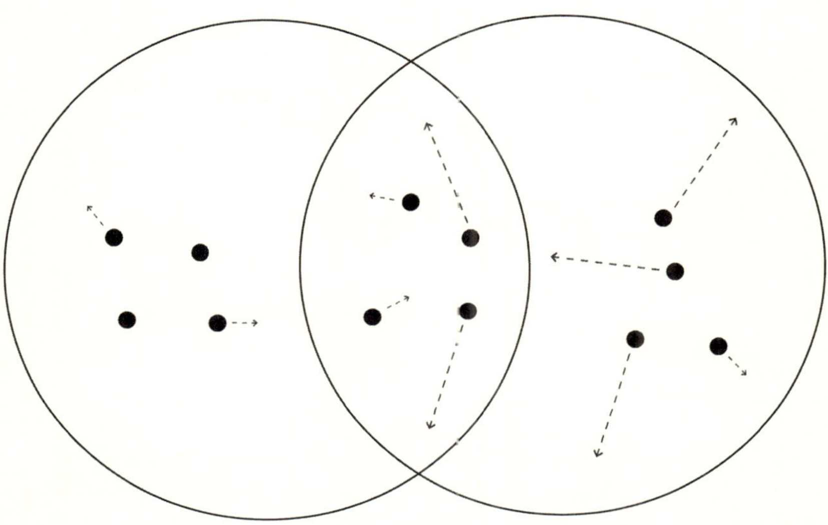

Between the gas and liquid states an area of overlap is
known as a phase transition

In moving between scales I hope to provide space for the reader or viewer to draw their own conclusions as to the role, existence and potential virtue of deviant behaviour.

As there will be a series of shifts in scale throughout this book, I would like to begin with an analogy between two radically different scales belonging to anthropology and physics: specifically, human evolution and a contained thermodynamic system.

In 1972, the American physicist and engineer Arthur Iberall created an interesting model that I believe can help us to understand deviancy[1].

1   Deviancy;
Arthur Iberall, *Towards a General Science of Viable
Systems*, 1972 p 288

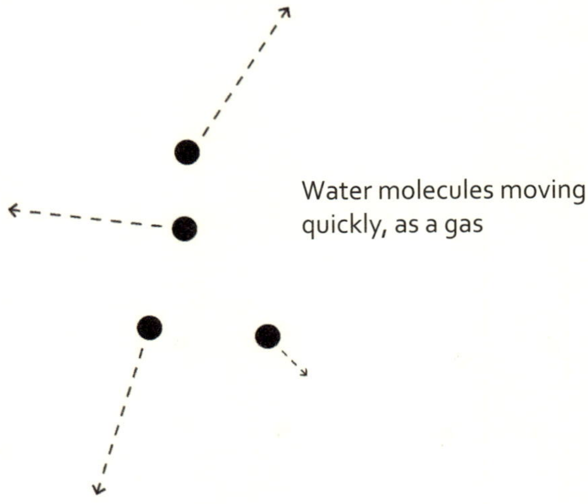

Arthur Iberall made an analogy between the molecular behaviour of water, left, and the organisational density of humans, right. As water is heated up it becomes more dispersed in molar organisation, akin to hunter gatherers.

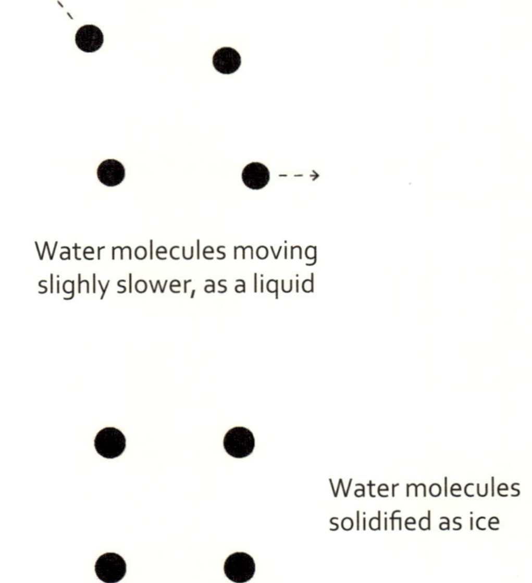

To complete the analogy, ice is structured by water molecules that are densly bunched together in a rigid state, analogeous to the urban sphere of the city.

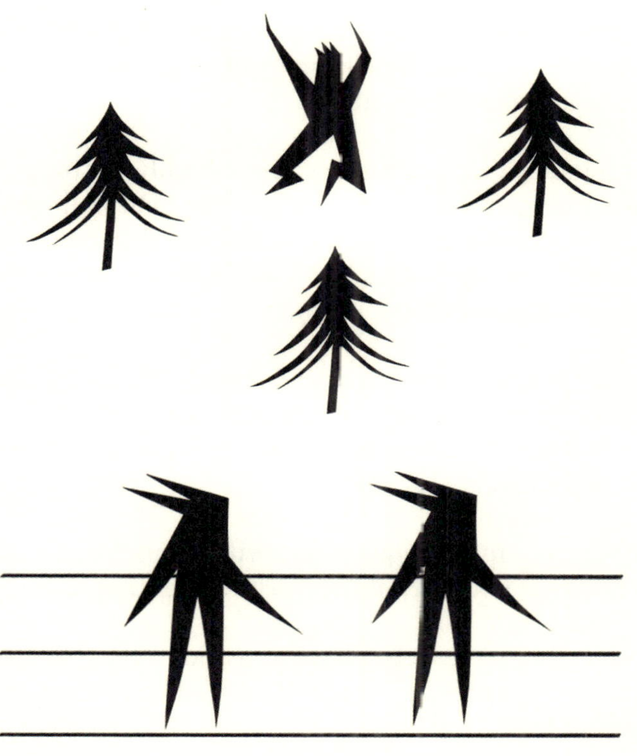

Iberall goes on to argue that the loose organisation of water molecules in their liquid state can be compared to humans during a period of agricultural production.

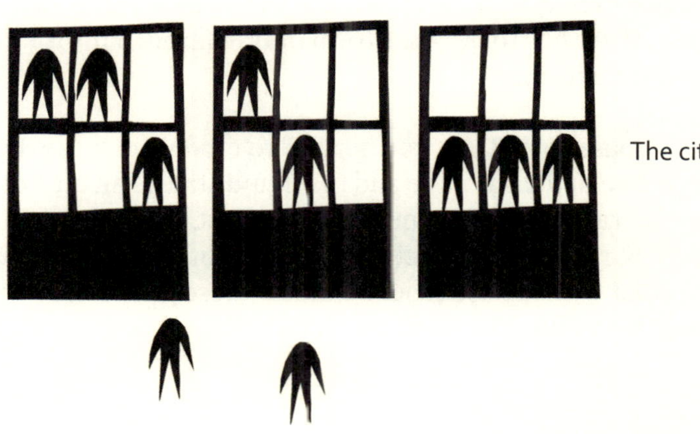

The city

The above model introduces the idea of a phase transition. I will use this model to describe deviancy through further diagrams and illustrations within this book.

This analogy is important because it highlights the potential to make arguments across different scales. The main problem with using abstract models to create real world arguments, such as whether to fear mass migration into Europe or not, comes from trying to jump across scales too quickly.

In order to move between models fluidly, I have tried to highlight a series of threads that draw coherent lines through the work. One of the analogical paradigms is scale, as I have begun to discuss, and another is language.

The scales of my argumentation will change from molecular to socio-economic to the regulatory institutions that attempt to govern subjects, materials and histories.
In each of these models, phase transitions, feedback and other physical properties have been identified and put into play against one another.

In the thermodynamic model above, I have drawn the structure of water molecules. These move differently depending on how hot they are. In fact, a water molecule's temperature is actually measured in terms of how fast it moves around. In standard physics, the greater the movement, the higher the temperature. Sometimes, as water molecules slow down, e.g. when moving from a gas to a liquid, there has to be some form of transition. This is known as a phase transition.

Phase transitions can be used to model deviancy. For example, between the gas state and the liquid state is an area of transition. In transitioning from gas to liquid, it is possible to measure the behaviour of water molecules. Any type of movement that is out of character with the usual behaviour of these gas molecules in their transition to liquid is 'deviant'. It is different, weird, and appears out

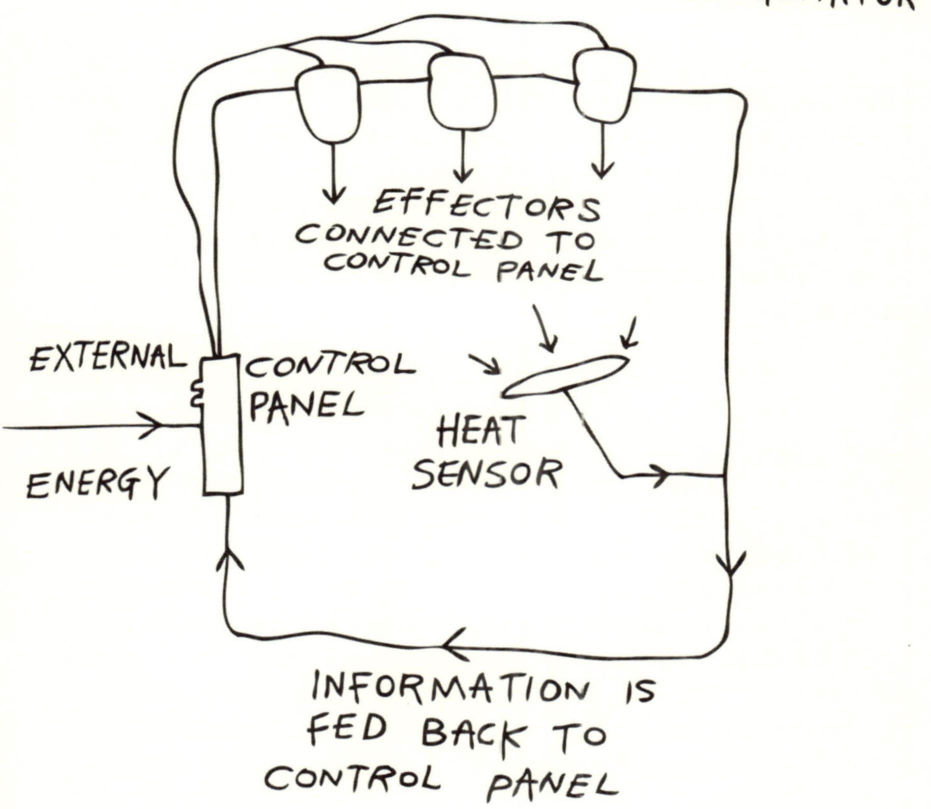

of place because it moves differently. Deviant behaviour can therefore be understood as an essential part of state change. Without deviation on the fixed form, no new form is possible.

The above *thermo-historic* model is a reference to: Arthur Iberall: *A Physics for the Study of Civilisations, in Self-Organising Systems, The Emergence of Order*, 1987.

There is one more term that I would like to introduce before beginning to explore art, magic and madness as forms of deviancy and deviant knowledge. This is the concept of negative feedback and it can also be modelled in simple terms.

The thermodynamic model I have drawn above is linear. One directional transformations of gas, to liquid, to solid are described for clarity. However, this could also occur as a cyclical process. In nature, gaseous water vapour, liquid water and ice do transform from one to the other in large cycles. In order to build a useful model I need measurable parts as I want to outline a scientific approach before commenting on what I think that approach shows us about deviancy.

Building on the idea of a phase transition I now want to introduce a new model. This second model will allow me to bring in the idea of negative feedback and this is important because negative feedback is all around us. Negative feedback is the process by which a system self-regulates. In the twentieth-century, feedback loops were arguably over-exaggerated to explain away highly complex systems into Ecology, Political Democracy and Cybernetics. For example, the British researcher and filmmaker Adam Curtis has highlighted the role of negative feedback in politics (known as Public Relations, PR). However, to avoid 'throwing the baby out with the bathwater', I believe feedback loops and abstract modelling can help us to understand the world and interactions between different systems.

In a refrigerator, a simple feedback loop known as negative feedback maintains a constant temperature. A sensor measures the temperature and feeds it back to the control panel. The control panel then uses external energy to adjust the temperature of the effectors. The effectors then act to stabilise the temperature of the system and the circle is complete. These processes are an attempt to prevent the onset of entropy and maintain thermal equilibrium (outlined in Chapter I).

If one thinks of the small changes in temperature within the refrigerator as phase transitions, it should already be possible to imagine how a more complex model could be built upon this simplistic diagram. For example, if I enter into a conversation, what I say will change the course of what is being discussed. It will not change immediately, but, over time, my ideas can be either be adopted by those in the exchange or not.

A less abstract example would be to imagine the formation and maintenance of a standard dictionary. Clearly, our use of words changes in subtle ways each year and editors of dictionaries are constantly selecting words to be integrated or deleted from the collection. New words are deviant to begin with, but if enough people say 'gumptyman' for long enough, it would become Standard English according to that dictionary at that time.

As I have approached each of my central subjects (art, magic and madness), my arguments invariably find their way back to language at some point: manifestos, magic spells, stuttering and even delirious non-sense. I have often (though by no means solely), framed my arguments in terms of language. In the cases of fine art and spiritual philosophy, the explicit limits of language are recurrent in my argumentation. To me, the grey zone of language highlights it as a living thing. Language has to be fed, worked and revised. However, in its very failure to capture 'the thing itself', language reveals a deeper knowledge of complex ambiguity. It is in this grey, living space of representation and communication that I conceptualize my artistic practice.

I will now try to draw a parallel to my thesis in the terms of its own construction. The text, in this instance, has been written in a linguistic interface many of us encounter each day: word processing software in computers.

In particular, the technology with which I have been writing this work has been attempting to change its content. Subtle errors made in spelling trigger the reflex of an autocorrect function that radically alters the words that appear on my screen. Coincidence? Ideological Conspiracy? Paranoia? Probably a bit of each; this form of content-shaping, computational algorithm has become normal[2]. Thus, 'have' became 'babe', (funeral) 'pyres' became 'tyres' and 'persecution' was corrected to 'perfection'. My own neologisms in *Here Comes Trouble*, such as *thermo-historic* and *scale parallax* are italicised. Words belonging to a standard norms of usage can be identified by the use of single quotation marks. Proper nouns remain capitalised unless they are being used to denote a standard norm, in which case they will also appear in single quotation marks, i.e 'American'.

If I were to list all of the words my computer has reflexively altered for me, over the entire period of writing, I might be able to create a model with which to analyse and study its behaviour. I like to think that, as a thought experiment, I can set a new precedent for the auto-correct, wearing the algorithmic programme down over time. Were this possible, a second set of data would emerge, and then a third; the words that I stubbornly re-corrected, and the ones the programme finally adopted.

The words that were neither correct in the first place, nor ultimately taken-on as the correct form, would constitute the lost product of my and the algorithm's little exchange. These lost words would constitute those that deviated from both the standard norm, and the new norm created by my usage. In this sense, then, deviancy can be understood as a model and its study a methodology: seek out the perverse or deviant and understand how it relates to the stand-ard norm.

As a model, I will assert that deviancy can be shown to occupy a certain 'morphologi-cal arena' between state changes within thermodynamic, social and cultural systems. Deviancy can therefore be conceptualised in terms of a transformation

2   Normal;
The idea that our minds should operate as high-speed data-processing machines is not only built into the work-ings of the Internet, it is the network's reigning business model as well. The faster we surf across the Web—the more links we click and pages we view—the more op-portunities Google and other companies gain to collect information about us and to feed us advertisements. Most of the proprietors of the commercial Internet have a financial stake in collecting the crumbs of data we leave behind as we flit from link to link—the more crumbs, the better. The last thing these companies want is to encour-age leisurely reading or slow, concentrated thought. It's in their economic interest to drive us to distraction.
Is Google Making Us Stupid? Nicholas Carr, The Atlantic, 2008

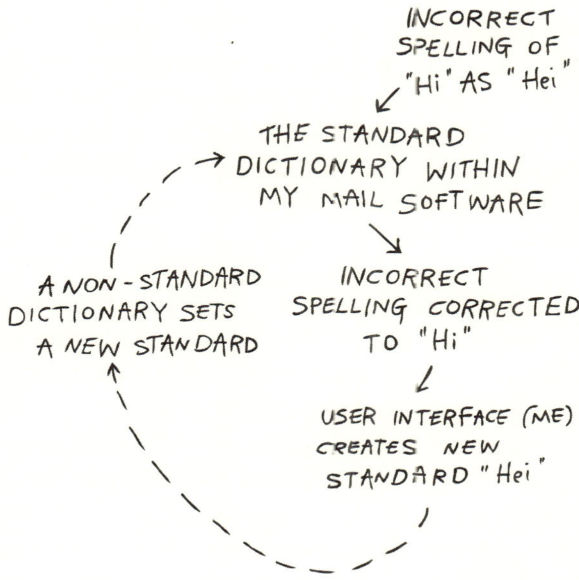

(from one stable state to another) as well as in relationship to stability (as that which deviates from the stable norm). Deviancy can then be measured as a form of behaviour that doesn't cohere or match with the given standard in its surroundings: we have deviant social agents and we have deviant or shape-shifting molecules. This paper will attempt to search out and identify the role of the deviant form within the morphological arena, so to speak, of different types of entities.

Insofar as the terminology can be trusted, I believe meaningful translations between the analyses of different types of structures (e.g. from water to social configurations) can be made, as is the purview of Systems Analysts. Systems Analysis or Systems Theory is a problem solving technique that separates a given system into its composite parts in order to understand how they function and enhance the overall system. Although this may sound a bit technical, weighing and comparing different things in an attempt to better understand them is characteristic of most human behaviour. We do it each time we cook, create and research. My work here attempts a specific form of research and analysis into deviancy. I have tried to explore deviancy's role as a given system develops toward and arrives at different 'stable states'. These can be social, chemical or cultural. The central model I would like the reader to keep in mind is that of the transition between the 'stable states' of water as ice, liquid and as a gas (vapour).

How can we measure the role of the deviant form during processes of stable state transition? The following steps serve to help identify my subject through the definition of specific terms, further outlined in Chapter I. Chapter I will attempt to clarify my terminology and raise questions. These questions will resurface and be addressed by chapters II and IV. Chapter III breaks my methodology by exploring some empirical research that is nonetheless directly related to my exploration of deviancy. The reader may work through II, III and IV in that order or read the text 'out of order' as II, IV, and III. Each chapter explores a model of deviancy within the paper using the methodological formula below, though not always in an entirely chrono-logical way.

(i) My initial task will be to identify an energy transfer between two stable states and an area of transition betwixt. Within an analogy that draws on political economy, in Chapter III, I have experimented by substituting 'energy' for 'agency', which creates a kind of bridge to the mysterious power of the money form of value[3].

(ii) I have sought to determine qualifiers for the terms 'stable state' in each thermodynamic, abstract spiritual and economic case, and the 'zone of transition' for each scenario.

(iii) It has then become necessary to elucidate on how and what the

3   Value;
'If we want to understand the social division of labour imposed by the market, we need to understand how an expansion of demand calls forth a capital inflow and an increase in the supply of the vast bulk of goods that can be increased in quantity by human effort.

...The only thing (two given) commodities have in common is that they are both objects of human labour. Obviously all real labour is the labour of particular types of worker, whether maker of coats or bus driver. As such they are examples of individual labour. They are also all taken from the general pool of social labour available to satisfy our needs.

A commodity is both a useful object, a use-value, and an exchange value. It contains a contradiction within itself. When it enters into exchange, the use-value of the equivalent serves to measure the exchange value of the other. The contradiction is not eliminated, it is reproduced on a higher level in the money form.

...This is exactly what we do when we weigh things. We know both the things we want to compare are completely unlike in every respect but one. To be comparable, they must have some common property. They both have weight (mass). There is no such thing as weight that we can isolate and measure independently of objects with weight. Likewise with value we can't just add up the quantities of labour congealed in the product at different stages of production. In the case of weighing something we start off by placing one object on a set of scales and finding it equal to the item on the other side, say a lump of metal. At a later stage, as we start weighing things regularly, we will probably ascribe a conventional measure to the lump of metal (for example ten kilograms).

...What we are doing in assessing value is essentially the same (as) we know both commodities are products of the pool of social labour'.

An introduction to Marx's Labour Theory of Value, *In Defence of Marxism*, Mick Brooks, Part One, 2002

4   'Normal' over time;
While focussing on the problem of 'how' these kinds of processes unfold, the treatment of the philosophical 'why?' must also be considered. The reader will therefore be warned that I intend, in several places, to drive toward the cliff of what it is conceivably possible to claim deviant knowledge, and its production to be. In this sense a *scale parallax* or vertigo, becomes necessarily apparent. Discussing an arena that is by definition, in transition between one state and another, between fixed meanings if you will, also necessitates that you and I occupy a slightly strange position from time to time. One that begs impossible questions so as to highlight the boundaries of knowledge production itself. Questions that may seem, at first glance, rather mad. This describes deviancy, not as we are used to conceptualising it, in criminological and sociological terms, but rather as an inherently creative, dynamic, even mystical aspect to the reformation of matter and new forms of life.

deviant form/s are, and in relationship to what.

(iv) Finally, in each chapter, I have asked what they, the deviant forms, do.

Again, I have chosen to explore art, madness and magic because each of these subjects involves a potential violation of what it means to be socially or scientifically 'normal'. However, as norms, rules and laws are subject to change, one might draw curves, diagrams and make models of trends and changes in what constitutes 'normal' over time[4].

In an age where pornography has practically become a public institution, North American rappers are openly homosexual, Radical Islam has become incorporated and state governance techno-monopolised, it would seem that the very idea of deviancy has been neutralised and contained. However, this is only because deviancy is understood as erroneous, folly or criminal. No matter what, deviancy is inherently tied up with forms of enquiry that involve transgression, diversion, the swerve of dance and play. Poetry, humour, carnal knowledge, left-liberal politics or the incommunicable trance of meditation: all posses an air of mystique. This doesn't mean that alternative forms of knowledge production are necessarily deviant; on the contrary, it is all too often assumed that they are. Nevertheless, some forms of artistic knowledge production can be understood as deviant, precisely because they don't attempt to produce anything. This point will be elaborated upon within an analysis of attempting to create a time share economy or Time Bank, con-

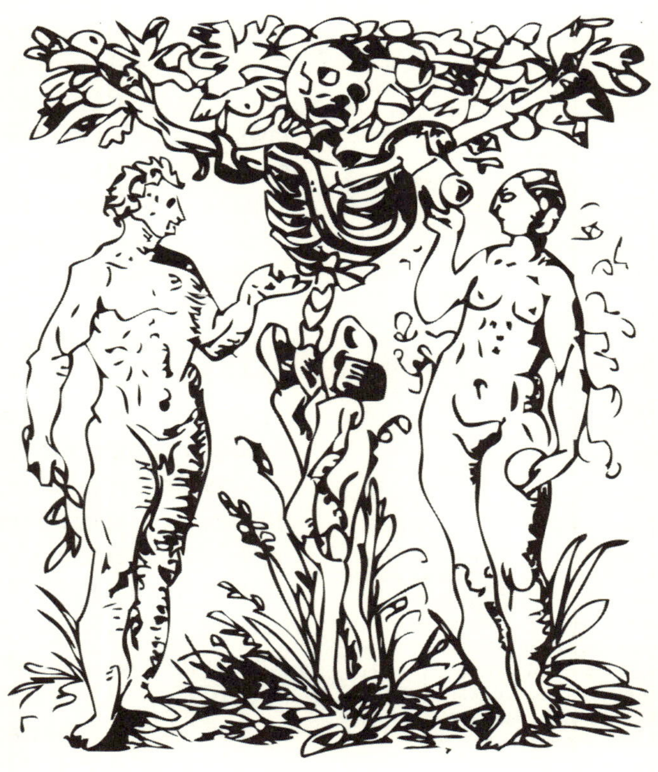

In Judaeo-Christian terminology 'knowledge' forms the epochal trade-off with paradise, be it carnal, intellectual or otherwise embodied. Here, a deeper possible meaning to the 'Tree of Knowledge' is illustrated as the transition of humanity from a vegetal form of being to the human as a living and dying vertebrate mammal. Note the snake alluding to the vertebral column or spine in this drawing after Jacob Reuff.

26

currently as both an aesthetic and socio-economic alternative in Chapter III.

Clearly the word deviancy has innumerable referents. In sociology, norms are composed of sets of social values that inscribe our moral sensibilities toward right and wrong. The failure of an individual to adopt such value systems may eventually push the tolerance of a given social group to its limits. The task of deciphering quite how social norms come to be created, how they change over time and are enforced, lies with sociologists, psychiatrists and criminologists. These social fields can also be illuminated through the lens of historical, philosophical and other discourses upon the notion of deviance. I may deviate from my thesis by smoking ganja. However, the act of smoking ganja, depending on one's social climate, may constitute another form of deviation altogether as the values of my environment will determine precisely what does or doesn't count as deviant. This explains the concept in ordinary sociological and criminological terms, which, perhaps due to a kind of practical necessity, explain deviancy through a binary relationship to its local counterpart, the social norm.

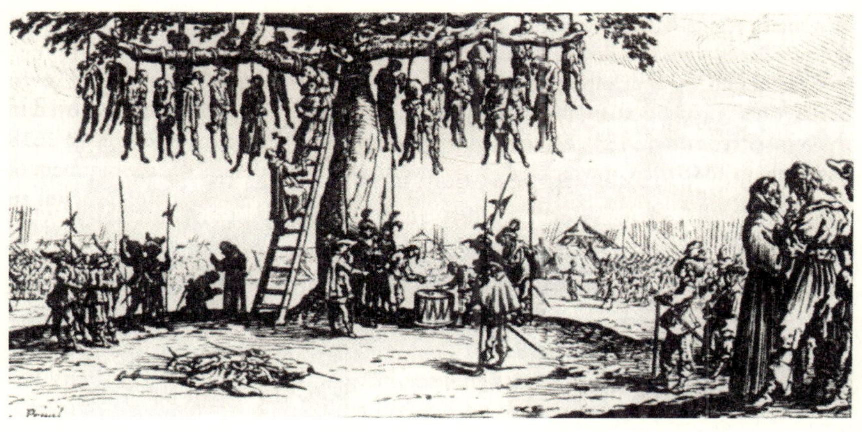

An alternative tree of 'deviant' knowledge: Jaques Callot, *The Horrors of War*, 1633, engraving. This image is liscensed under the Creative Commons Attribution-Non-Commercial 4.0 International Liscense, sourced from Silvia Federici, *Caliban and the Witch: Woman the Body and Primitive Accumulation*, 2004.

It will be the task of this paper to explore the role of the deviant form within differing sets of social and material processes and, ultimately, draw conclusions about the production of new knowledge itself as either mad, inspired or scientific. What might deviant knowledge look like today?

In some spiritual disciplines, knowledge itself is understood as a distraction, not to mention its deviant form. More accurately, the concept of knowledge within spiritual disciplines is really spiritual knowledge, while thought per se acts as a distraction from Dharma or cosmic order. For many of the religions stemming from India such as Hinduism and Buddhism, the waking world constitutes a surface, Māyā that defrauds one of access to spiritual understanding. In Daoist philosophy the pursuit of spiritual understanding constitutes 'the way', a powerful path toward ultimate enlightenment delivered through a spiritual bond with the universe. Ideas, surface impressions or thoughts are, to these doctrines, energy caught in a cycle of life and death, caught in mind. In this mystic reading, all knowledge is perverse, and everything we do with it, build with it, the wars we wage for it and the hierarchies within which we repress it, represent the transgressive agency of human endeavour.

It follows that as a human, and not a rock or a chair, my agency is born from consciousness. No matter the extent of my material power today (as a human rather than a squirrel), in the first instance, for Aristotle, man is a 'reasoning creature'. [5] I have the responsibility of choice, however trapped and perhaps a little awe struck at my own facility with tools such as language, as I may be. Spiritually, we could say that language comes at a kind of cost, and that that cost is a displacement from 'home' itself, both in a primordial sense and in a cultural sense also.

Through displacement [6], suspicion and the fight for survival, fear would seem to be irrevocably tied to deviancy in social terms. It is the pursuit of this paper to make the term more ambiguous, to highlight deviancy as kind of analytical tool in itself, partly because it's fun, partly to reflect on ways of understanding social anxiety,

5   Reasoning creature;
For the anthropologist David Graeber, whose work will be
discussed below, measuring and comparing things, one
against another is primary to what humans do.

 Salam! Hello! In the coloured text of the book I have developed a parallel narrative that attempts to discuss the issue of migration, cultural belonging and difference. Throughout the work, the reader will find thoughts that bridge my research into deviancy and migration.

In Judaeo-Christian terminology 'knowledge' forms the epochal trade-off with paradise, be it carnal, intellectual or otherwise. I always find it amusing when the ultimate symbol for this anxiety, the bitten apple of Apple computers, is covered up like the proverbial fig leaf of Eve, along with the mythological roots of the Garden of Eden.

This anxiety toward the condition of a 'knower' pervades throughout the doctrines of hate, guilt and enslavement that constitute my cultural background, only deeply submerged. As a post-colonial Brit, born on an island and now living on the mainland, a specific space is reserved for worrying about 'otherness', too. Amidst a tableau of intermeshed cultural textures, xenophobia must be an acute discomfort to those for whom belonging is inherently dependent upon cultural belonging (rather than spiritual).

For nationalists, some cultural signifiers promise fixed, eternal meanings, such as the national flag, traditional food and ideological narratives of glory and conquest. If these established tropes are set against the cultural opportunism of a globalised world economy the latter soon fades in comparison. In short, culture 'easy come', threatens to also be culture 'easy go'. This is a valid concern - only, it is one I would level at the cultural dilution of markets and not at 'foreigners'.

Parallel Narrative

but furthermore as an acknowledgement that an infinite pulsing, rotating, shrinking and expanding morphology is the reality of the universe within which I exist. Deviant knowledge production is simply one way of describing this morphological process. Equally, there will -by definition- be limitless other ways of describing and modelling deviancy.

If 'attachment breeds suffering' as Buddhists teach, perhaps we can understand the xenophobic nervousness associated with 'alien cultural practices' as inherently bound up with the very alien-ability of what passes for contemporary culture. Logically enough, in other words, if I can belong anywhere, I belong nowhere.

As the front lines of the wars raging in the Middle East draw closer for the West, this is an anxiety that increasingly performs as a double helix between 'manmade climate change' (in so far as it creates displacement), and 'globalisation' (in so far as it articulates displacement) - the two, apparently inescapable, conditions of our era.

Deviancy is related to belonging in so far as, historically speaking, those groups that migrated and set up camp then ac-cused anyone who did the same of being trespassing 'aliens'. It was customary from time to time, to draw a line and say, this is us and anything beyond that line constitutes another category. To deviate in this sense is simply to wander, to walkabout, and to do so is to discover oneself as just such a migrant soul. Yet death remains a real possibility to long distance migration and this detail does somewhat close down the romantic scope of the wandering, deviating poet. However, the virtue of understanding deviancy on multiple scales (thermodynamic, cultural and others) is that the deviant form can be located within larger cycles of material transformation. Fear of the unknown is certainly a part of how the term deviant is ascribed. When the mind becomes stuck on a phrase or argument with anoth-er we can so easily become distressed. Once acknowledged as only a part of the story we tell ourselves about ourselves, a fear too can become a less troubling entity.

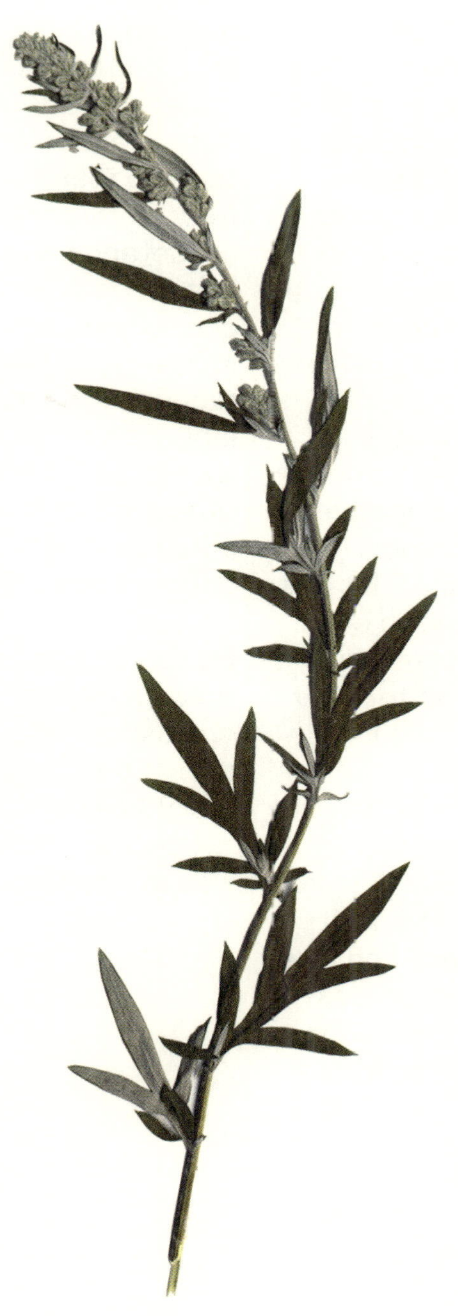

Here Comes Trouble is frankly something of an understatement. With the current demographic shifts taking place in Continental Europe and across the Middle East, foreign difference threatens to become re-politicized as deviancy anew. This work is a call to understand how the concept of deviancy works, what it might mean, and to neutralize its negative, undifferentiated socio-political ascription. This has been necessary with each developing era of left-liberal, humanitarian thought. The problems of the left, and, for the right, of there being a left, will not go quietly into the night. Deviancy is a contentious subject to model, bordering, as it does, the 'criminal' and (the more prosaic) 'otherness'. In turning my mind toward this problem, the shadows of its potential immensity and the implications of freshly racialised discourses across the world, have been made explicit.

Is it curiosity or doubt that leads to our undoing? Projections, doubts and desires are often used as tools to foster a culture of fear, moral panic as well as metaphorical and literal 'witch hunts', both of which concern me here. Once a McCarthyite inquisition redefines the meaning of language on its own terms, the scope for claiming that others are participating in criminal, deviant thought is dangerously unlimited.

History has set a troubling precedent; first comes enclosure, then the ascription of deviancy. Those who resist likely find themselves the bearers of this dubious title in one form or another.

Parallel Narrative

Clarifying an Analogy Between the Study of Physics and Alternative Scales

The sun

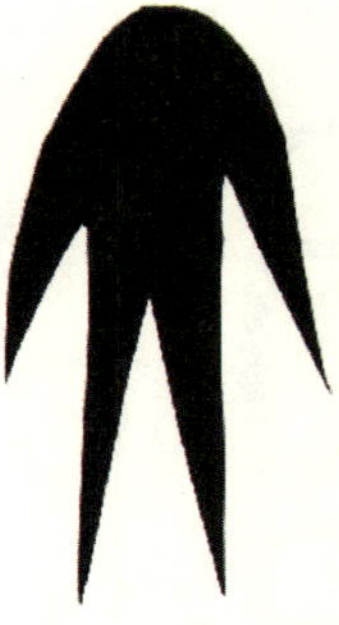

Medium sized human

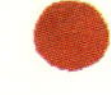

Silica atom

Meaningful discussions of anthropological analysis appear to be made available by the study of physical models such as thermodynamics. However, let me draw back for a moment. Something is being prepared and it would not do to rush. Is it really appropriate to discuss social phenomena such as deviancy in the context of thermodynamics? Manuel DeLanda would say yes. And, arming myself against brazen equations, I would have to agree. My faith can be explained in two ways: by my assertion as a reasoning adult that when comparing the literature available, a certain level of agreement has been reached upon the scientific terms established and from my political experience of people, money, energy and organisation.

The following basic structure has allowed me to approach larger quantities of information and reach deeper into the subject of deviancy.

Testing my Methodology 1:
Thermodynamics of boiling water

In this example I will attempt to establish the basic principles outlined in my introduction and begin to discuss what deviancy might mean in terms of entropy. In this example:

(i)   Energy is transferred in the case of liquid water molecules becoming vapour through the application of heat.
(ii) Two 'stable states' can be identified as the 'water state' and 'gas state'. The point at which water transitions into gas, i.e. its boiling point, represents the zone of transition.
(iii) At this zone of transition water molecules exhibit deviant behaviour in the way they move about, occupy different positions and react to one another.
(iv) The more stable molecular behaviour of water deviates into that of gas, causing an increase in molar activity and an expansion of the overall space needed to contain the system.

Negative feedback plays a crucial role in the thermodynamics of an open system such as a refrigerator. An external energy source is used to maintain equilibrium and prevent entropy or decay. Yet for a closed system, such as the human body, no amount of external energy can prevent the onset of entropy.

The term entropy comes from the Greek 'energy' + 'transformation'. The most general definition of entropy is as a measure of uncertainty about a system.

As a physical problem, entropy is a measure of probability. The easier it is to predict a molecule's behaviour, the lower the scientific measure of entropy. However, the statistical mathematics used to measure entropy has produced many other lines of questioning.

The terminology of thermodynamics also leads to some confusion: is it 'chaos' or 'disorder' if my predictions become less accurate? Is entropy good, bad or ugly? As I will try to argue, the physical measurement of entropy and our philosophical responses to it affect the way we approach life and the notion of 'progress'.

The artwork of the American minimalists such as Donald Judd, Carl Andre and Robert Smithson, for example, allude to multiple readings of entropy. Their work is fascinating to me insofar as minimalism sprang up precisely when statistical analysis hit a big bang (the computational modelling of the late sixties and seventies that shaped the world we know today). This computational modelling is also known as 'systems theory' or 'information theory' (from here on, systems theory) and artists like Robert Smithson were early to voice their critique.

On the whole I would say entropy contradicts the usual notion of a mechanistic world view. In other words its a condition thats irreversible, its a condition that's moving towards a gradual equilibrium and its suggested in many

ways ...Buckminster Fuller also has a notion of entropy as a
kind of devil that he must fight against and recycle.
...In information theory you have another kind of entropy.
The more information you have the higher the degree of
entropy, so that one piece of information tends to cancel
out the other. The economist Nicholas Georgescu-Rogen
has gone so far as to say that the second law of thermodynamics is not only a physical law but linked to economics.
He says Sadi Carnot could be called an econometrician.
Pure science, like pure art tends to view abstraction as
independent of nature, there's no accounting for change or
the temporality of the mundane world. *Abstraction rules in a
void, pretending to be free of time.*

Robert Smithson, *Entropy Made Visible*, Interview with Alison Sky, 1973,
The Writings of Robert Smithson, 1979 (authors emphasis)

Smithson then goes on to refer to entropic processes of global
proportions involving the depletion of natural resources such as oil
and gas. It is not clear whether a direct link is being made for Smithson between the statistical analysis of entropy within gas and water
and the statistical analysis of what he calls information theory.
Smithson uses a notion of time. For him, abstraction knows its truth
only in a fabricated void 'pretending to be free of time', revealing
disillusionment with humanity's treatment of the finite resource
of Earth. Ironically, such weighty materialism smacks of American, seventies boom-bravado but there is something more subtle,
more cosmic to Smithson's endeavours as a body of work. His most
famous work, the Spiral Jetty, 1970, apparently lost for a period
following his untimely death, can be understood as an unravelling
material philosophy in itself. It remains ambiguous as to whether
the Great Salt Lake is being sequestered by land or, more excitingly,
perhaps the entire landmass of the Americas is simply a transition-
al, tectonic 'stable state'. It is worth making a definition here: there
are no true stable states for hard science. The term is useful however, as a way to define a set of circumstances and conditions from
which to elucidate on how things might work. In grasping great
minimalist artworks, I sense a series of allusions to the infinite
stretch of time prior to and following my own contemplation.

Mystics have often meditated on the relation of the human scale to both the tiniest molecule and the size of our solar system as a whole.

I believe one should view Smithson's works as situated within a very large scale of time indeed. In order to do so, one must also cultivate a sensitivity to what is required in the now. 'Presence', as it is discussed in spiritual discourses, is crucial to reading Smithson's minimalism and to reading the way he is approaching the problem of entropy. Only a series of moments constitute our trickle of time in this world, thus the only thing that is ever meaningfully taking place is occurring now. If I can grasp this, presence provides an insight into the agency of the moment; it gives me both the energetic impulse to move (matter) and the finite condition of life (an interweave of energy and entropy). This is what gives minimalism its urgency.

Testing the Methodology 2:
Autocorrect

(i) Energy is transferred in the case of human labour to new knowledge through work.

(ii) Two stable states can be identified as: the formal dictionary a given word program uses to correct mistakes and the revised dictionary which then includes any new words adopted after repeated use.

I would identify the zone of transition as the back and forth of mistakes, correction, rejection of correction or agreement between a word processing program and myself.

(iii) The deviant forms here are words such as 'Adata' being corrected to 'data' or discrepancies between the Americanised spelling of 'specialised' to 'specialized' depending on the program.

(iv) What does the deviant form do? It forces norms to adapt,
which, in turn creates new deviations. Neologisms (new words)
come into existence in order to express new experiences. Specifically, in this scenario, they also serve to reinforce identity
through atypical usage. By challenging them, the autocorrect
function is also sifting out those that can be lost and those that
mean something to the writer. The process by which an autocorrect program establishes a new, stable idea of what to correct and what not to correct is an example of negative feedback.
The simplistic characteristic of norm creation and therefore
new deviations cannot really encompass the complexity of,
for example, a social system. However, taken together, these
models do create a lens through which to view deviancy and a
very specific lens is required for this task as deviancy is always
on the move!

As with the refrigerator diagram on page 19, negative feedback is the aspect of a system that tells it how to effect change in order to increase stability. In the example of an autocorrect program, an algorithm serves to stabilise the writer's output into a given standard. Words, officially recognised, standard English ones, are sorted in or out through the information fed back when an autocorrect is either overwritten or stabilised. Or should that be 'stabilized'? To me, in each of these cases, a trend can be observed whereby processes of feedback attempt to control and organise divergent sets of elements or material, be they energetic or linguistic.

One could argue that any system of communication requires a set of standards in order to function. At its core the above example highlights the acceptance of an essentially arbitrary set of rules that have only become socially enshrined as such over time. Though it is understood that spelling is an application of sounds and shapes to objects and experiences, it is the systematic setting of standards that works to the immense benefit of a body of knowledge. Within my inquiry into deviancy I have often observed a drive to move heaven and earth by first ensnaring meaning within the regulatory apparatus of words, laws and ideological reasoning. If I trace my own assertions of meaning to the infinitely transitory, language (thought broadly as a system of communication) presents a kind of paradox: no thought escapes language; yet, as a set of truths, language is without substance.

The 'entropy' of an autocorrect programme is hard to imagine. Perhaps it could be measured by thinking of the Internet as a huge linguistic machine. In a sense, the linguistic entropy I am imagining has been confirmed by the Oxford English Dictionary 'word of the year' award going, not to a word but to the crying (with laughter) face Emoji, as referenced by writer Hannah Jane Parkinson on the Radio 3 programme *Free Thinking* in 2016.

All matter, ourselves included, passes through cycles of constitutional change. I have introduced the idea of entropy that, for physicists, is associated with the amount of order, disorder or chaos in a thermodynamic system.

However, I want to be clear about my conceptualisation of entropy and equilibrium before bringing in my historical examples of deviancy. The concept of entropy is tied up with the second law of thermodynamics. Any closed system will be affected by entropy and inevitably becomes un-structured, chaotic and collapse. Rotting food is a visual example. If food is left without the external energy of a refrigerator to artificially maintain its thermo-equilibrium, entropy brings it to decomposition.

Similarly, your body, could be considered a closed system undergoing a process of entropy. Maintaining its thermo-equilibrium is of key importance to its survival. Without external energy plugged into it in the form of food, the molecules of your body, currently organised in forms of relatively homogeneous stability, or sameness, will, dissolve into an unstable, heterogeneous pool of differentiated parts.

The differences within this pool of matter can be measured at different scales and in different ways. We can measure differences in chemical and behavioural terms and by the manner in which each element interacts with the other elements in its environment. This is another way of describing the practice of systems theory that was established in the mid twentieth-century.

Yet it is also important to recognise that entropy and equilibrium have different meanings in different contexts. These multiple meanings can create some confusion so I will try to be explicit. Equilibrium simply refers to the overall sameness of a group of entities. These could be molecules themselves or the way molecules are behaving. Thermodynamic equilibrium means that all the molecules in a closed system (like boiling water) are moving at roughly the same speed.

However, equilibrium can also mean the final resting point at which all competing forces are balanced. Therefore when a living system decays into un-structured mush one also refers to the structural equilibrium of matter. Entropy is the process by which matter succumbs to equilibrium over time. The relationship of thermal energy (heat) varies depending on the system being studied.

Taking your mind from the question of heat or movement for a while, I want to continue discussing the idea of entropy and some of the challenges that have been made to this apparent law. Illya Progogine, for example, has challenged the second law of thermodynamics, stating that it only holds true for closed systems. When a system is open to interactions with diverse flows of energy and material, the number of outcomes and the degree of entropy exhibit unpredictable new behaviours.

Nonetheless, entropy remains the second 'law' of thermodynamics. Think of this as minimalism's first critique: if everything leads to decay why the big fuss of global consumerism? Surely the ostentatious architecture of the late twentieth-century is simply an oil fuelled, short-sighted mistake? What is 'progress' if it will all end in chaos and collapse?

Definitions of entropy according to Robert Smithson, Taken from *Minus Twelve*, Robert Smithson (1968):

2   ENTROPY

A   Equal units approaching divisibility.
B   Something inconsistent with common experience or having contradictory qualities.
C   Hollow blocks in a windowless room.
D   Militant lazyness

However, as mentioned above, in the 1960s the Belgian physical chemist Ilya Prigogine, and others discovered that the law of entropy is only true for CLOSED SYSTEMS[1].

According to Prigogine, entropy is not a given for OPEN SYSTEMS with energy and matter flowing in and out. These discoveries opened up the idea for non-linear modelling including demographic and market forecasting[2]. However, one could argue that this kind of reasoning then gave birth to a new type of hubris: the age of computer driven societies. This is where I find an additional critique within minimalism: we may think that statistical probability mathematics will show us how to optimise society, politics and economics in order to keep change and chaos at bay, but we need only look at the world around us to recognise that the very opposite has become true. In the short term, new models and systems are geared towards producing results that show economic predictability and growth. This may be because when shifting scales, for example between ecological systems and economic ones, it is easier, in the short term, to hide *entropic bugs in the system*.

The act of modelling entails a degree of generalisation and abstraction. The simplification, classification, and organization of data into types, causes and effects allows for a mechanistic conception of the world easily fed into computers. By ignoring entropic deviation, or at least creating self-regulating classification feedback loops, these models are not just descriptions of reality but also attempt to prophesise it.

Therefore, this is a trait that has been inherent (or perhaps more explicit) within capitalism and its expansion since the fifteenth-century when slave labour was abstracted into goods for waged workers in Europe to consume, and fulfil the projected never ending upward growth curve. However, the evidence presented in this paper shows that the entropic history of deviation is often left out of these modelling processes. The treatment of the mentally disabled and the execution of women as witches are testament to these *entropic bugs in the system*.

1   Closed Systems;
Ilya Prigogine and Isabelle Stengers, *Order Out of Chaos: Man's New Dialogue with Nature*, 1984 p 20

2   Forecasting;
Adam Curtis, *All Watched Over by Machines of Loving Grace*, 2011 part 1

Though the capitalist application of systems theory and computational economics has survived, it has only done so at immense human and environmental cost. As a means to deliver new, more prosperous solutions to the worlds' needs, systems theory has, largely, failed. So, my work here is an attempt to place systems theory at the disposal of those made vulnerable within processes of socio-economic upheaval. On a theoretical level, I believe I have achieved this goal through identifying an area of transition experienced by migrants, asylum seekers and refugees upon entering a new socio-cultural environment. This idea is detailed in the conclusion to the parallel narrative found within this book [3].

In my mind, systems theory with a keen eye to the role of deviation can be used to meaningfully enhance our comprehension of complex sets of events. In so doing, a sharper set of analytical tools may be developed with which to understand transitions from one stable state to another, and the behaviour of large and complex systems.

By introducing models of positive and negative feedback, a nonlinear historical model situates agents and events within cyclical processes of morphological change. Without a non-linear conception of history the investigation of morphological areas of change would be impossible.

I have already begun to describe deviant behaviour within nature in somewhat abstract, scientific terms. In order to grasp the building blocks with which to assemble and reform the component parts of my argument in Chapter II I will attempt to explain particular social phenomena and courses of events using an application of thermodynamic modelling from Arthur Iberall and Manuel DeLanda.

The work of Manuel DeLanda has been crucial to bringing these ideas into play and his work *A Thousand Years of Nonlinear History*, (1997) will be discussed in detail in the following chapter.

These insights have then been applied to the treatment of the mentally ill during the late Renaissance to late Classical period of Western European history. I have made specific study of the treatment of mental illness documented by the French philosopher-historian Michel Foucault and I have also focused on the lesser-known narrative of women executed as witches during the same historical period by activist and historian Silvia Federici.

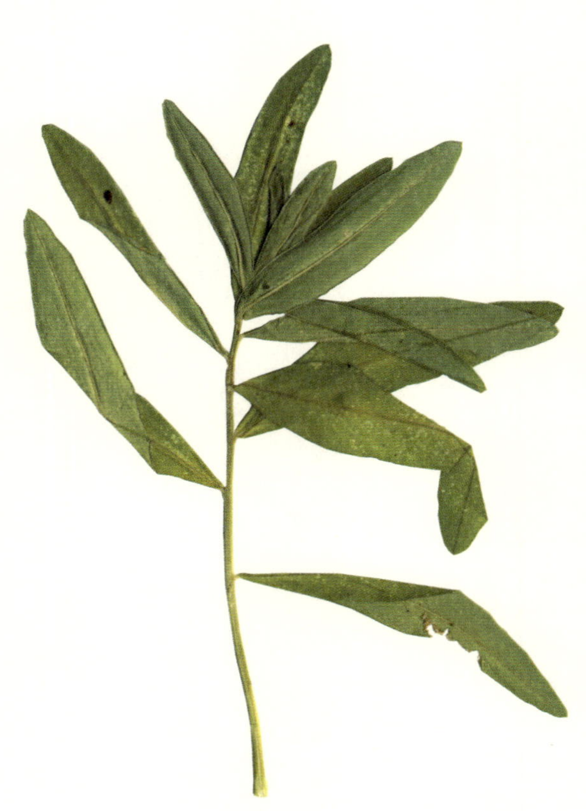

3 Materially grounded in socio-cultural terms, my ambition is to apply these insights to contemporary attitudes toward social deviancy. As stated in my introduction, reviewing and discussing deviancy is important because spaces and personages deemed deviant are by their very nature under threat. One could potentially employ the theoretical apparatus developed here as a type of first person, qualitative research. This describes a potential crossover whereby a theoretical work of systems analysis can be used to substantiate sets of approaches, attitudes and practical research. Systems theory has long been used to advance predictions about vast processes of on-going change. These have proven limited and there are of course moments when active engagement trumps speculative knowledge production. Though complex ideas may require complex tools from time to time it doesn't take a clairvoyant to hear an urgent call for new forms of intercultural/linguistic hybridisation within Europe. In the face of an advancing European Right, the opposition will always need to voice its arguments through multiple voices and languages. Groups such as the Jugend Theatrebüro (Youth Theatre Group), Berlin-Moabit, which have consistently brought together every possible demographic; vulnerable, indigent or 'German' persons for the past seven years lead the way. Search for Jugend Theatrebüro, Berlin.

Part One of a Meaningful Scale Parallax: Discussing Deviancy in Relation to Homogeneity and Heterogeneity

This chapter can be read using the following methodological formula, as outlined in my introduction. However, the reader should be warned that the methodology is in fact drawn across two chapters. As an interstice, I have included the review of empirical research into what I am referring to as deviant knowledge production in Chapter III. This empirical research has been conducted in the form of an aesthetic and socio-economic alternative, the Schuldkröten-syndikat. You are encouraged to read these chapters in the sequence that suits you best. This chapter contains parts (i) and (ii) of the following methodological structure:

(i)   Heterogeneous or 'mixed' elements in the form of localised producers are gathered around the energetic impulses of early-industrial mass manufacturing. Energy is transferred in the case of non-hierarchical markets to regulated markets through workers' efforts. I will first use the example of early markets to illustrate the manifestation of markets as a stable state before looking at a more powerful process of consolidation, the regulatory institution.

(ii)   Stable states emerge in the form of markets, here, from the late medieval period within Western Europe onward. As regulatory institutions develop through processes of negative feedback, so too do organising criteria for citizens. The zone of transition in this analysis is the shift from non-hierarchical market meshwork's to stratified institutions of regulation. This study of markets is done in order to establish a historical background to the spatial investigation that will follow in Chapter IV concerning Michel Foucault's *Madness and Civilisation* and Silvia Federici's *Caliban and the Witch*. Here, the sorting criteria that create a zone of transition have been determined by shifts in the emerging European economy. The zone of transition will therefore be a complex amalgam of economic tolerances toward the labour required by the market, an individual's tolerances toward a capacity to work and societies tolerances toward those who cannot work.

(iii) By tolerance one might also read: sympathy towards or capacity to bear the weight of, depending on ones' political outlook. As sorting criteria become specified and formalised through legislation, further consolidation occurs; deviancy to a given market's stable states becomes coupled to those unable or unwilling to contribute to emerging manufacturing processes (either out in the world or at home). Indeed, as practical measures of social control step in to handle or 'treat' the unemployed person and the itinerant woman, to be unable to contribute to the economic reproduction of the period (or to be unable to work) is to be 'mad' or to be a 'witch'. Finally (in further exploration of the role of deviant speech in Chapter IV), the reaction of societies toward madness or unreason will be measured by the capacity of the mentally ill to master language itself.

(iv) What, then, does the deviant occupy herself with? Spirituality? Gardening? Revolutionary politics? Poetry? Magic?

<u>Cast</u>

If this paper were a script, the main speaking parts would go to three central characters: Silvia Federici, Michel Foucault and Manuel DeLanda.

Silvia Federici is a long-standing feminist activist and professor of social sciences. She is known in left-wing circles as one of the first activists to critique the debt-mechanisms established by the International Monetary Fund (IMF) in the 1980's. Federici currently teaches in New York City. Michel Foucault is an esteemed French philosopher and historian of ideas. Intimately concerned with the dialectic between our corporeal, and psychological worlds, Foucault's seminal work, *Madness and Civilisation: The History of Insanity in the Age of Reason* (1961), provides the proverbial plot structure for this chapter and Chapter IV. Acting as broker between the worlds of art, philosophy and science, is the Mexican-American artist and philosopher Manuel DeLanda. All three of these authors aim to make historical ideas available through their work, though none more so than the robust portfolio of Federici, who, as I will draw on in this chapter, represents some highly disenfranchised share-holders.

Each of the above authors foster and develop ideas with which to change the way we exist in the world, born from material and socio-political analysis. They develop ideas with which to understand complex historical situations as a series of holistic relationships often interwoven with fear, greed and repression.

Deviancy, in this chapter, is coupled to the historical parameters discussed within Foucault's *Madness and Civilisation: A History of Insanity in the Age of Reason*. In keeping with Foucault, it is the dramas of these sequential periods of invention, discovery, and enlightenment and modernisation that concern me here. The rigorous work of Foucault immerses the reader within the transition from classical to modern attitudes toward the mentally disabled.

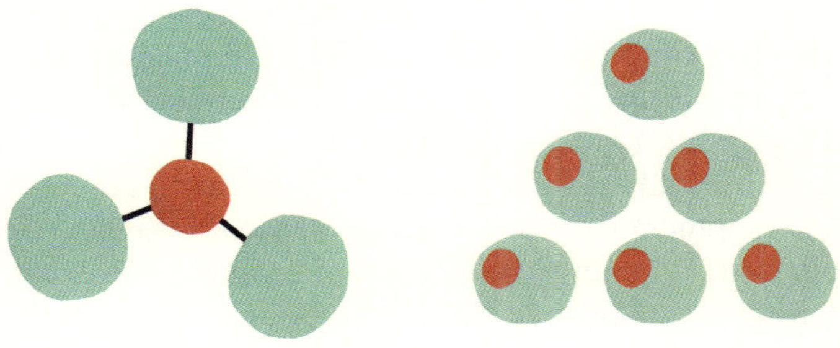

Federici's dedicated project to rewriting Marx takes the ramifications of this time period a step further by revealing the affects of primitive accumulation on enslaved and female bodies. These interesting times are further textured by the fundamental churning historical pragmatism of *A Thousand Years of Nonlinear History* (1997), (hereafter, *A Thousand Years*), by Manuel DeLanda. A work that attempts nothing less than the systematic analysis[1] of Medieval Europe onwards, DeLanda places his 'thousand year subject' under the philosophical microscope of the physical sciences. Interactions between bugs, bacteria and burgeoning colonial European empires coalesce within *A Thousand Years*. They coalesce in a manner characteristic of other scientific ventures into the simulation of natural systems[2] yet with none of the pretence toward autocratic omnipotence so often present in the official historical record. In order to employ this methodology to the work at hand, concerning social norms and their deviant counterpart, my endeavours, too, require that I begin with a multiplicity of 'things' on display.

The impact of newly mobilised resources and the technological developments, through which those resources were to be employed, lies at the heart of what Manuel DeLanda refers to as the emergence of 'autocatalytic loops' of 'self-sustaining groups' within Western Europe. In the models used by DeLanda, strong influxes of energy represent the point at which a given system is pushed from equilibrium, resulting in diverse linear and nonlinear historical outcomes. It is possible to locate the manufacturing shifts identified by DeLanda, within late medieval and early classical communities, as paths of developmental deviation based on material-resources, human labour and fuel-energy transfers. For example, the extraction of slave labour power from African nations, built the cities of Bristol and Liverpool in England. Parallel to this exploitation, landowners began to extract wage labour from newly enclosed farmlands across the European continent during the fourteenth and fifteenth-centuries. Again, analogously speaking, there are clear parallels to thermodynamics when we conceive of the events triggered by access to new materials, fuels or technologies.

1, 2 Systematic analysis, Natural systems; 'By the late 1960's …our modern idea of nature, the ecosystem, and cybernetic theories about computers had fused together. Out of it had come an epic new vision of how to manage the world without the old corruption of power. It was a vision that seemed to be different from all past political attempts to change the world because it was based on the natural order. In 1967 a young writer named Richard Brautigan crystallised this. One morning he walked through the streets of San Francisco handing out a manifesto. It described a future world held in a balanced equilibrium by the fusion of nature and computers. It was called All Watched Over by Machines of Loving Grace.' Adam Curtis, *All Watched Over by Machines of Loving Grace*, 2011 Part 2, For an extensive critique of totalising theories such as Economics, Science, Ecology and Cybernetics, search for Adam Curtis's work.

Market Consolidation

As energy enters into a system, sequences of events, both linear, one-directional transfers, and non-linear, cyclical processes are triggered[3]. From a strictly *thermo-historic* point of view, the wholesale manufacturing, urban and industrial transformation of Western Europe during the late medieval, renaissance and early classical period, represents an enormous movement of energy. Analogous to this particular *thermo-historic* narrative runs the historical fog of social sensibility and class dynamics, in short, the relationships forged and broken by the tensions of political upheaval. The interweave of religious fear and human desire, with new economies of scale across new territories, substantiates a complex assemblage that, I argue, would result in a material impact upon both the human mind and body political. The role of the church, aristocracy and state to secure the hearts and minds of its citizenry would become ever more closely tied to the interests of an emerging economic power base, increasingly composed of the merchant class and landed gentry[4].

Nonlinearity

In order to sufficiently dismantle or unpack the dense mesh of these interwoven scenarios, artists, philosophers and historians have demonstrated the virtue of abstract diagrams born from the study of thermodynamics. The artist-philosopher Manuel DeLanda, who has drawn on the abstract machines of Gilles Deleuze and Felix Guattari (philosopher and psychiatrist-activist, respectively), demonstrates the pitfalls and virtues of systems analysis of this kind. In the nonlinear model developed by Ilya Prigogine and drawn on by Manuel DeLanda, negative feedback performs the function of stabilising a thermodynamic system.

3   Triggered;
Manual DeLanda, *A Thousand Years of Nonlinear History*,
1997 p 14

4   Landed gentry:
'Under the newly emerging capitalist order, the logic of
money was granted autonomy; political and military power
were gradually reorganized around it. True, this was a financial logic that could never have existed without states
and armies behind it in the first place.'

David Graeber, *Debt The First 5,000 Years*, 2011 p 321

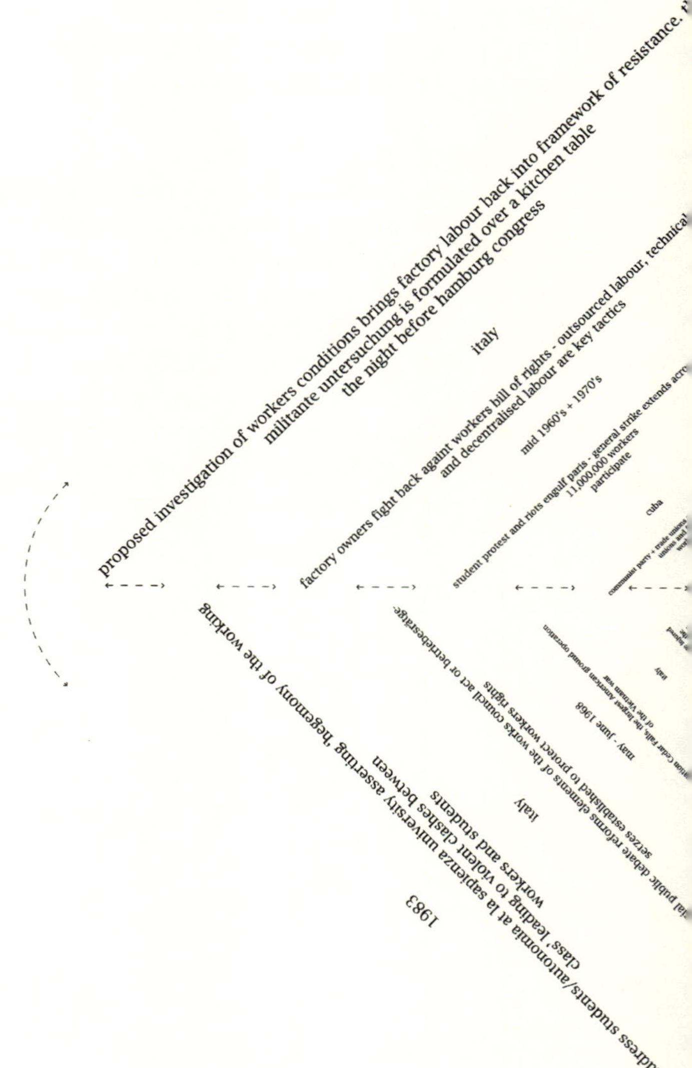

proposed investigation of workers conditions brings factory labour back into framework of resistance. t...
militante untersuchung is formulated over a kitchen table the night before hamburg congress
italy
factory owners fight back againt workers bill of rights - outsourced labour, technical and decentralised labour are key tactics
mid 1960's + 1970's
student protest and riots engulf paris - general strike extends acro... 11,000,000 workers participate
cuba
communist party + trade unions / unions and ...
italy
...nists address students/autonomia at la sapienza university asserting 'hegemony' of the working class', leading to violent clashes between workers and students
1983
italy
...al public debate reforms elements of the works council act or betriebsrate... seizes established to protect workers rights
may - june 1968
from Cedar Falls, the largest American ground operation of the vietnam war

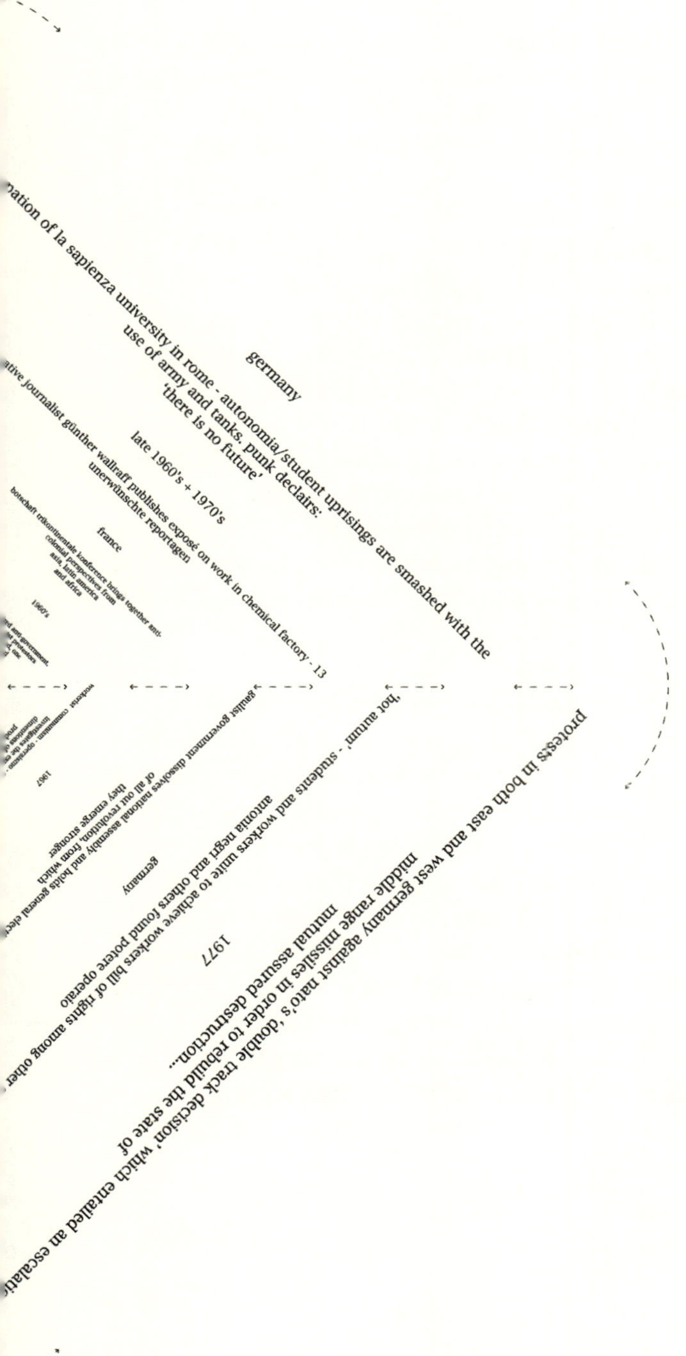

...ation of la sapienza university in rome - autonomia/student uprisings are smashed with the use of army and tanks. punk declairs: 'there is no future'
germany
late 1960's + 1970's
...ative journalist günther wallraff publishes exposé on work in chemical factory - 13 unerwünschte reportagen
france
botschaft trikontinentale konference brings together anti-colonial perspectives from asia, latin america and africa
1960's
...d anti-government ... protesters
workerist communism - operaismo ... investigates the ... they emerge stronger
1967
gaulist government dissolves national assembly and holds general elect... of all out revolution, from which
germany
antonia negri and others found potere operaio
'hot autumn' - students and workers unite to achieve workers bill of rights among other...
1977
protests in both east and west germany against nato's 'double track decision' which entailed an escalat...
middle range missiles in order to rebuild the state of mutual assured destruction...

Introducing an abstract diagram of negative feedback gives us an insight into how geological, organic and socio-cultural systems self-regulate. To witness the function of self-regulation, in turn, illuminates how the deviant form behaves during a system's pursuit of stability.

The interaction of novel expressions and self-regulation demonstrate and permit a cyclical rather than linear course of events. Though there is no final thermodynamic equilibrium of entities within the universe, negative feedback differs from its 'positive' counterpart in that the latter involves an accumulation of reactions and counter reactions. The model of negative feedback for the medieval market system is the regulatory institutions that seek to sort and stabilise. The (in)famous big economic bang of the Reagan and Thatcherite years involves precisely the removal of these forms of regulatory measure, allowing for the exponential boom of what turned out to be synthetic investments and the debt bondage of the Global South (and North)[6].

I will explore the relationships between nonlinear modelling and markets below. Manuel DeLanda is interested in making analogous arguments between thermodynamic examples and social and historical phenomena, in so far as these models allow us to transcend a linear view of historic processes. To sympathise with a teleological, linear conception of history is, in this view, to ignore larger, cyclical processes of global and cosmic transformation as nature and humanity strive toward apparent 'progress'. One way to understand nonlinearity is through the natural sciences. Clearly, for DeLanda nonlinearity also offers a meaningful critique of the capitalist labour relations, insofar as a critique of the accepted notion of human progress is really a critique of the scientific, technological and moral 'progress' bound up with hyperacceleration of capitalist systems of organisation.

<u>The Market as Meshwork</u>

In order to shape the analogies I am attempting to draw between DeLanda and, later, Foucault and Federici, I will now open up the idea that markets, particularly rural or early, medieval ones, contain a series of 'things' on offer that correlate to other scales of heterogeneous masses that go through consolidation processes, with a particular focus on the example of granite.

6   Global Debt, South and North;
Adam Curtis, All Watched Over by Machines of Loving Grace, 2011 Part 1

Image on pages 60-61: a nonlinear historical timeline. I first began to work with the idea of nonlinear histories in 2014, producing two timelines with the programmer Patrick Kochlick for an exhibition titled *Merchant Cities*, The Substation, Melbourne. Those works are referred to as 'Schematic'. They are narratives simplified in the manner of electronic diagrams that display only the essential, functional components of circuitry. However, a new way of handling the problem of nonlinear timelines (histories that require concurrently abstract thought and the retention of new information) is in order. Moving toward more representative historic modelling, I would encourage the reader to think of this paper as a set of proposed diagrams for a new series of programmed, non-linear timelines. *Here Comes Trouble*, could, for example be a set of socio-historic scenarios, a kind of dramaturgy that can be played in a variety of orders over and through one another. In any case, I have a fascination with the capture, distortion and reproduction of new knowledge that could take many forms: visual, aural or, in this case, historical and theoretical.

Meshwork Model
of Ingneous Rock

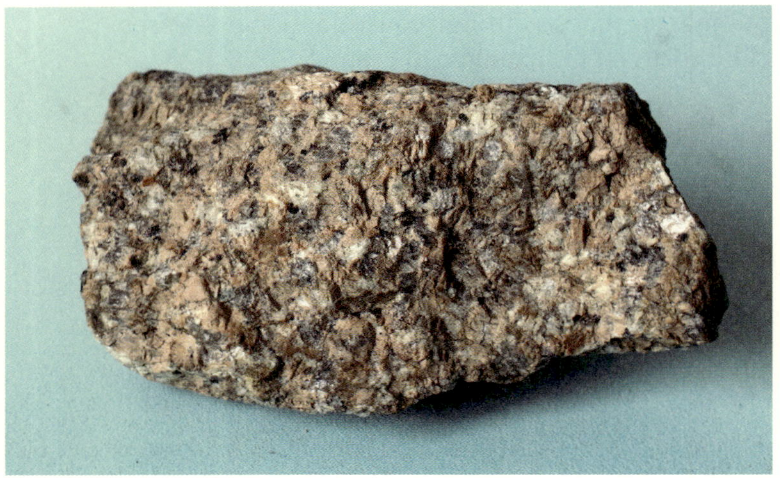

A sample of igneous granite donated by an assistant at the Natural History Museum, Oslo

The igneous rock granite is composed of a meshwork of different, heterogeneous elements. Each of these elements that are visibly differentiated to the naked eye are, in fact, different formations of the same base material: silica. Different chains or compounds are categorised as different polymers.

Meshwork Model
of Ingneous Rock

My specimen contains the following minerals with the corresponding
structures that I have modelled to
the right.

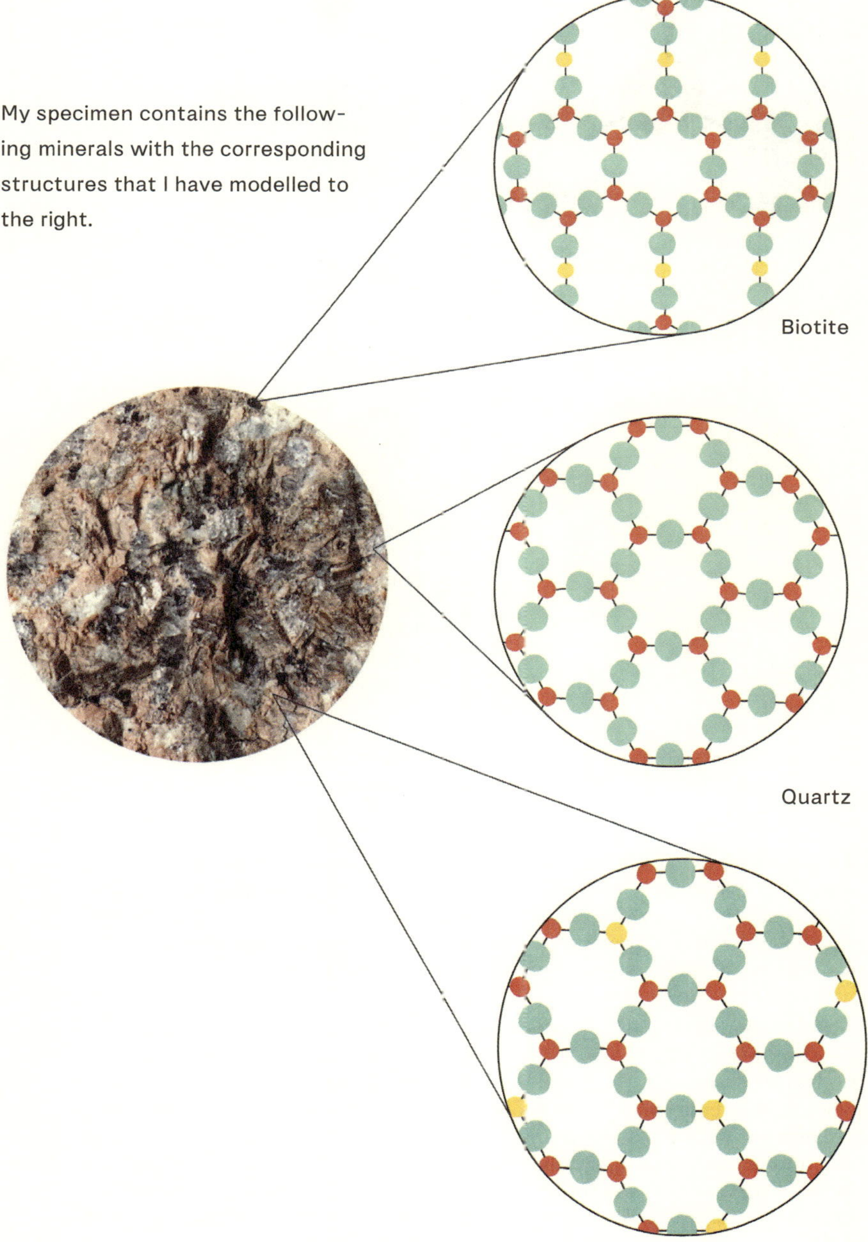

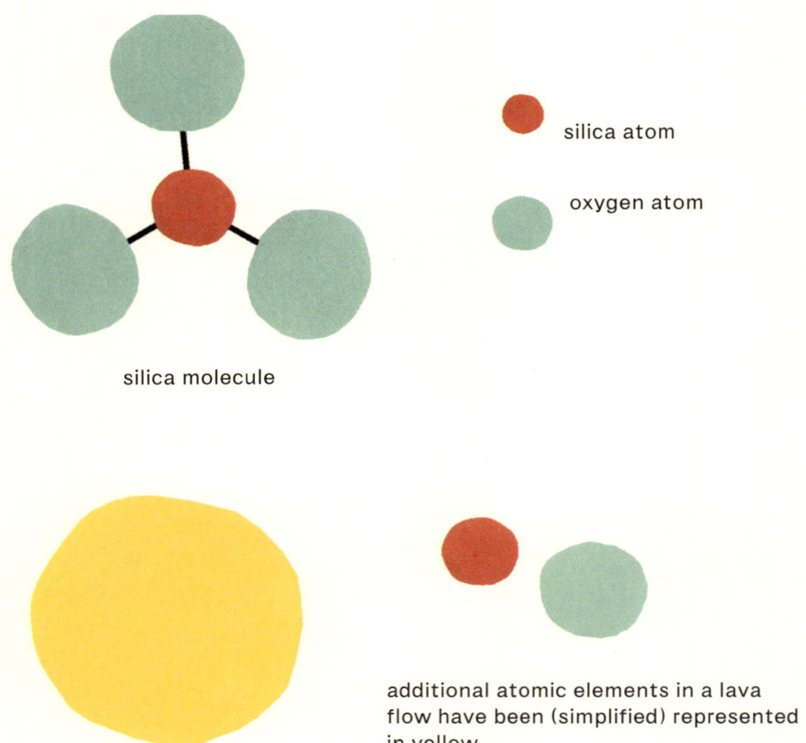

Silica molecules are composed of 4 oxygen atoms and 1 silica atom. I am using a simplified, two dimensional model showing 3 oxygen atoms and 1 silica atom.

Additional minerals such as magnesium, iron, aluminium and others are also part of molten lava. These are important for the interlocking of chains of molecules within the formation of the minerals feldspar and biotite. For simplicity, I am using one colour, yellow, to signify these additional minerals that act as catalysts within cooling molten lava.

These 'impurities' to the most homogenous formation of silica (quartz), function within a complex overall process called fractional crystalisation as magma cools. Only from studying these material processes have I been able to comprehend the theoretical terminology adopted by Manuel DeLanda such as his description of 'intercalary elements'. These 'elements' are, upon closer reading, actually both material atomic structures and ,in a sense, events within the formation of granite meshworks. A secondary intercalary element for DeLanda is the intermixing of different magma melts which both trigger and interrupt crystalisation processes.

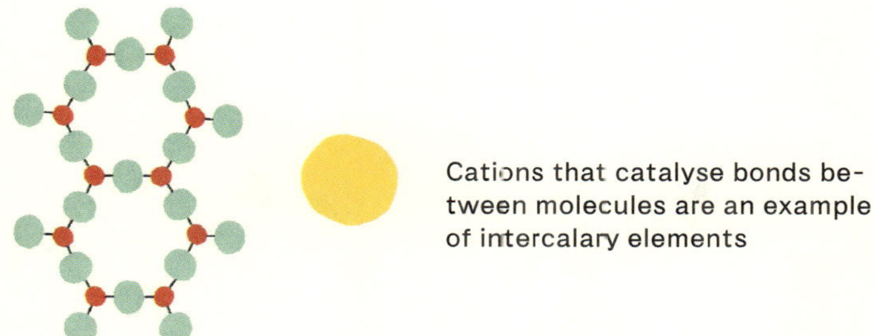

Cations that catalyse bonds between molecules are an example
of intercalary elements

Bonding elements such as aluminium and calcium
serve as 'cation' connectors within biotite and k-
feldspar

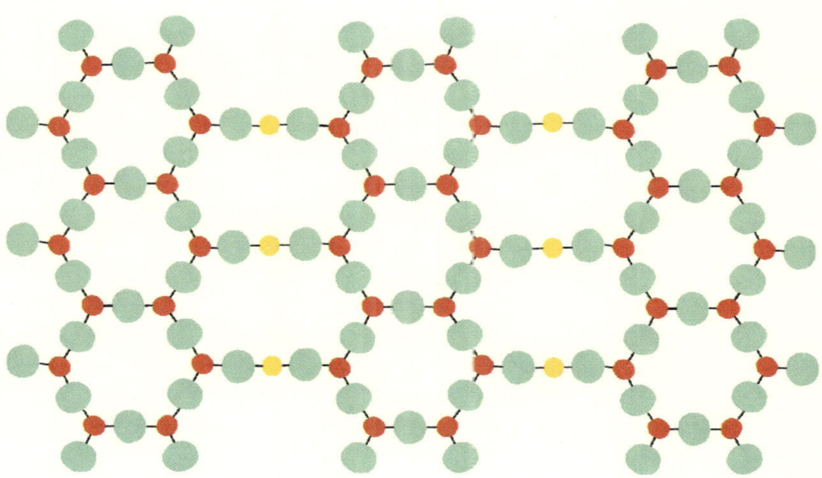

Biotite chains are bonded into sheets

K-feldspar

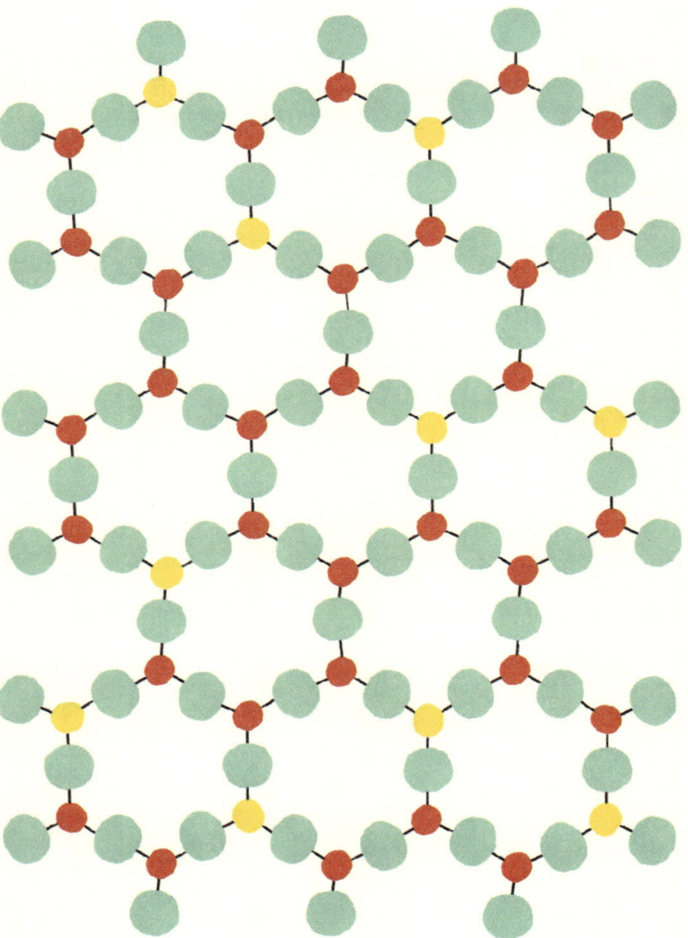

Crystals with interchangeable 'impurities' are different from larger, homogeneous structures of atoms and molecules. In their case, larger molecular structures can only bond by using (the positive or negative electronic charge of) additional elements such as magnesium, iron, calcium or aluminium. Thus the silica formation k-feldspar is a heterogeneous composite of aluminium, calcium, oxygen and silica atoms. Unlike biotite, which uses these cations to bond chains of biotite molecules, k-feldspar is an intrinsic compound. K-feldspar forms into a network structure by balancing its electronic charge through a more complex bonding process than biotite or quartz.

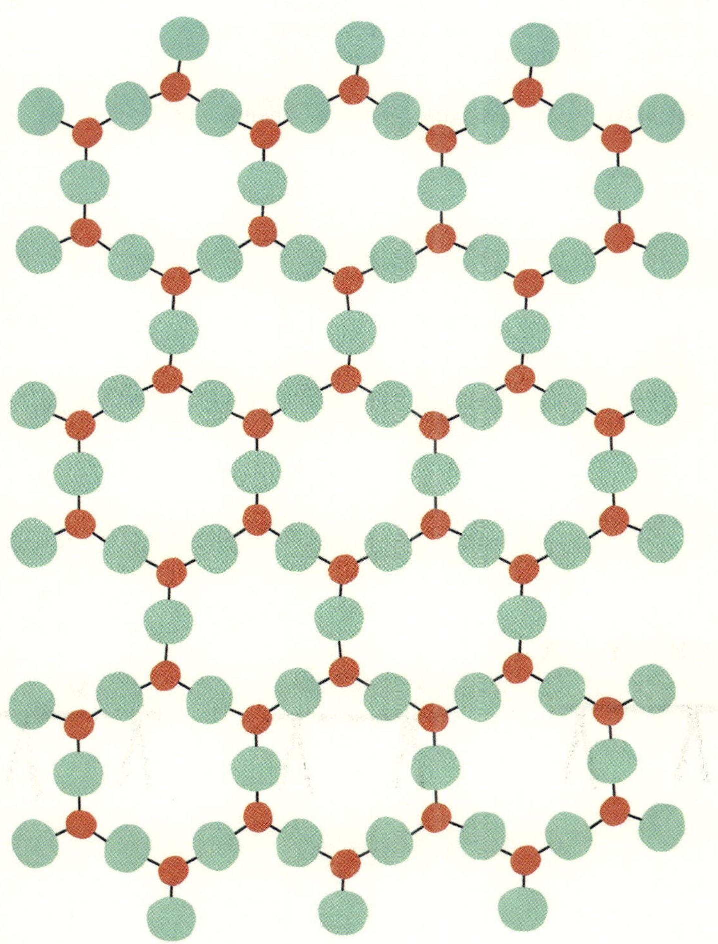

Quartz – The most common form of crystallised silica, quartz, is organised in a framework structure. A pure, hexagonal bonding sequence is created by all four of the oxygen atoms of silica being shared within the overall structure.

The Price Mechanism

For Manuel DeLanda the price mechanism of a late medieval market is another expression of an 'intercalary element'. The setting and flexibility of relative value through a price mechanism facilitates the exchange of goods and services, across a great heterogeneity of things on offer at the market

A late medieval market contained a great mixture of goods and services. I refer to these as 'things'.

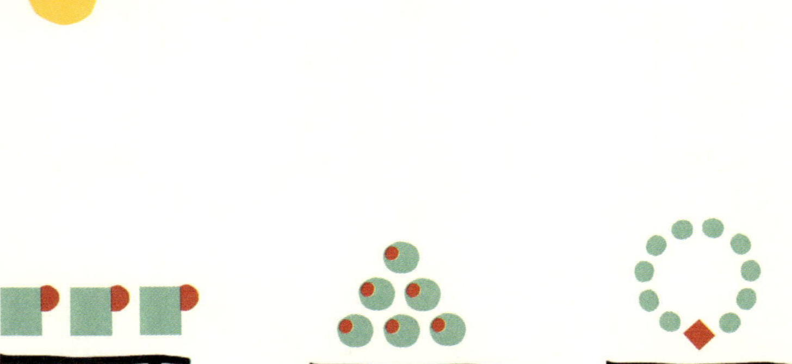

Sales are made possible in relation to the market's consensus evaluation of each 'thing'. For DeLanda, this was how a multiplicity of exchanges were catalysed before monopolies and price fixing shifted market dynamics.

The Price Mechanism

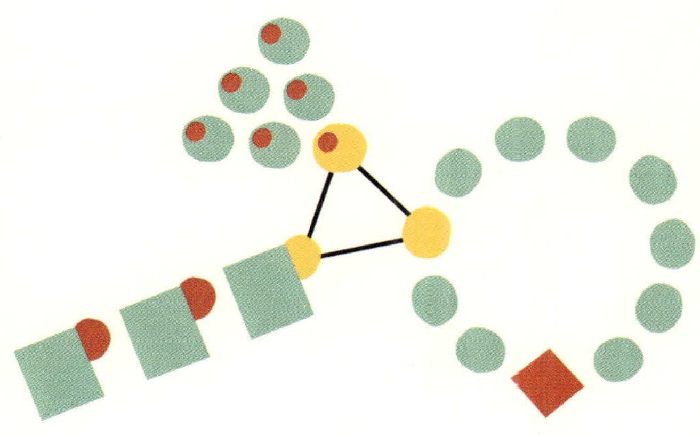

For Karl Marx, the value of an object or service is only revealed at the moment of exchange. Therefore a price mechanism, the use of money (or, more often, credit) allows for the flow of goods between hands without the need for direct barter.

When an object is exchanged its use value and its exchange value determine its worth, e.g how many cups for so many olives. By using a pricing system, a great multiplicity of needs, offers, goods and services can form into complex temporal meshworks analogous to the formation of igneous granite rock.

Here, too, the intercalary element, now the price mechanism of the market, facilitates bonds and further growth. This growth and stability is measured by DeLanda in the regularity of markets held throughout a circuit of towns or villages. Ultimately, the expansion of medieval markets created a tissue of rhythmically synchronised prices that would come to fluctuate across Europe in unison.

In this sense, an exchange through the consensus price of the overall market represents different forms of value; that which gives it use value or exchange value ...but something lacks in this analysis. As markets grew in scale to the huge multinational corporate infrastructures of today, objects began to tell us less and less about their creation. Who made this fine necklace? I will very rarely know. Thus the capitalist mode of exchange hides one crucial aspect to the creation of an object's value: labour.

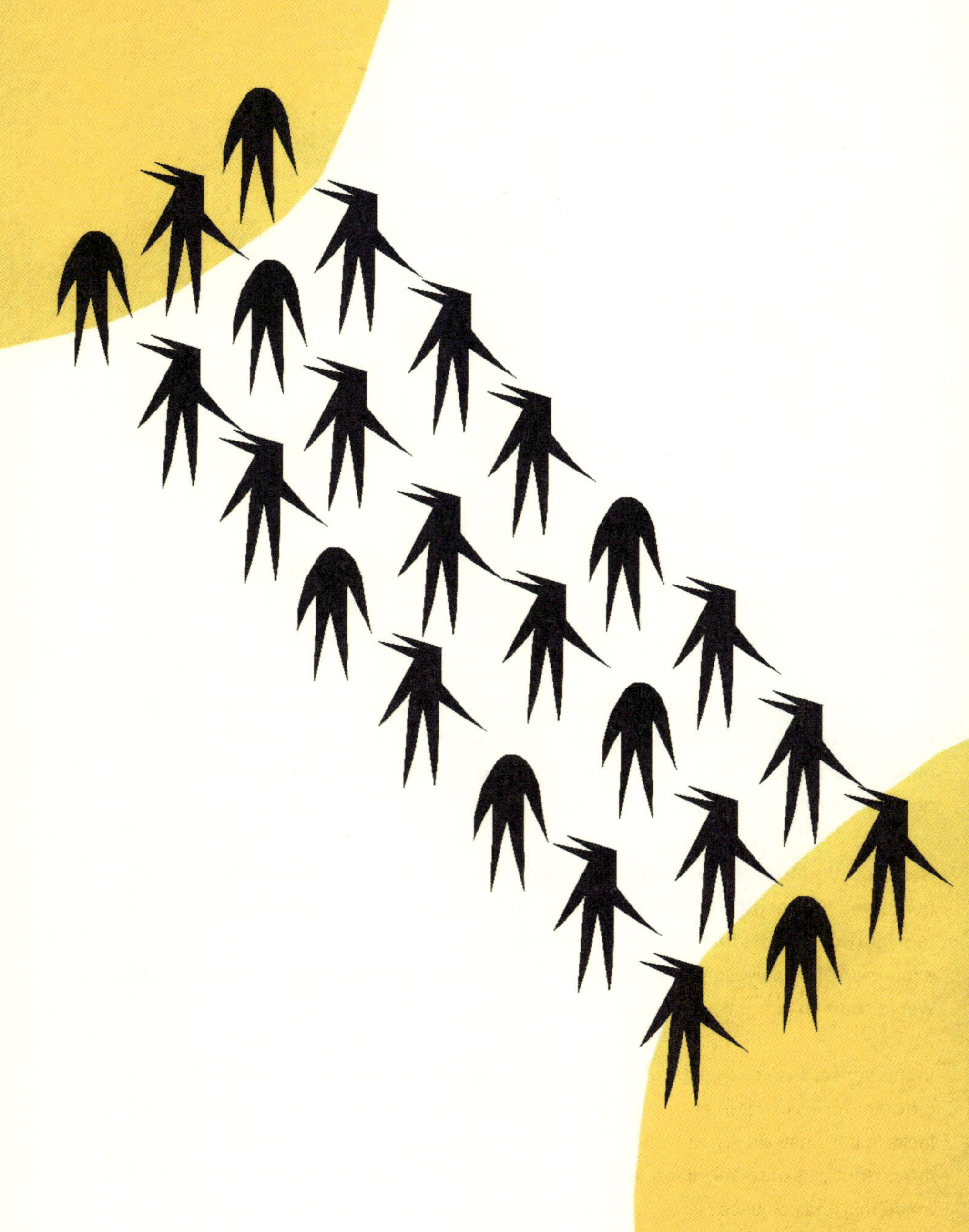

Emergence of
Regulatory Institutions

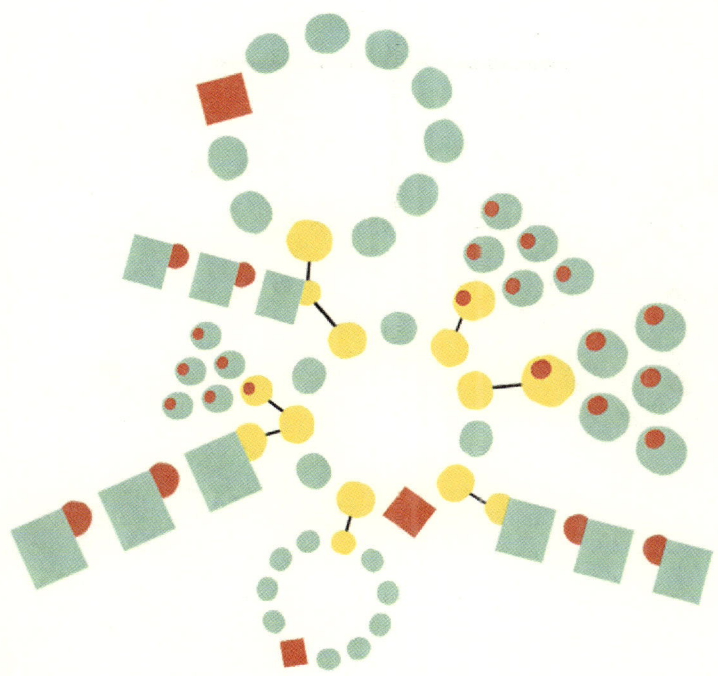

As markets become increasingly complex, regulatory institutions emerge acting as a secondary catalyst to trade.

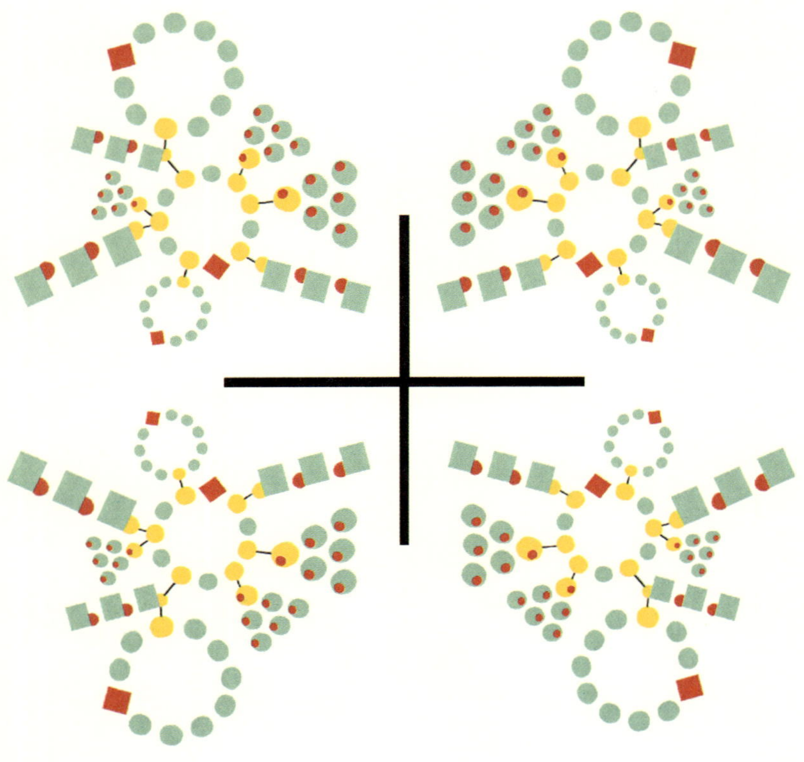

I am using the interface between horizontal forms of organisation, such as late medieval markets, and vertical hierarchies of organisation (such as the church or markets with a pure money market above other exchanges), to represent the emergence of regulatory institutions.

The rise of institutional departments of regulation (organisational bureaucracies, whether for markets, military expansion, legislative or medical purposes) has been widely documented within Europe from the fourteenth-century onward.

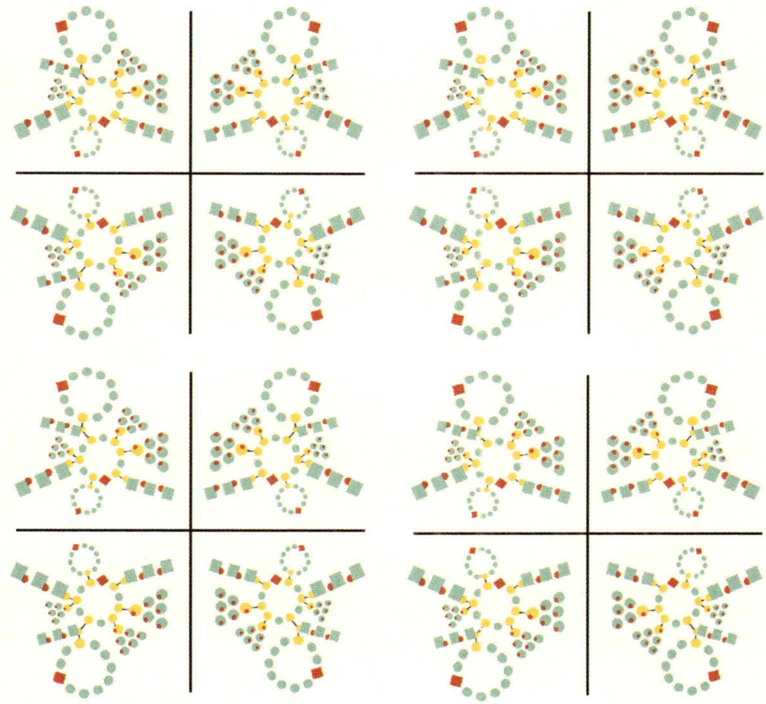

Meshworks, characterised by de-centralised decision making
continue to intersect with hierarchical systems of organisation
up until today. As these societal and economic traits became
more and more complex, so too did the institutional apparatus which served to channel these awesome flows of energy
throughout Europe and the wider Islamic and far Eastern worlds.

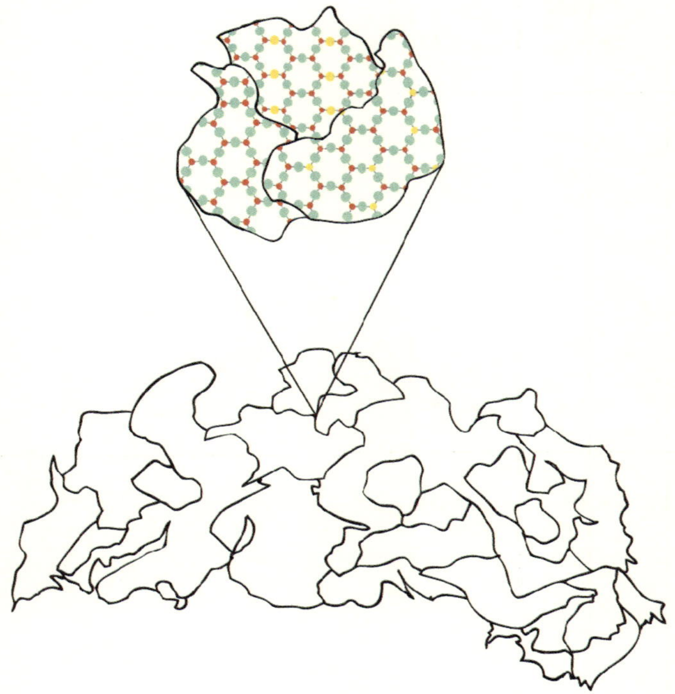

A solidified chunk of granite has passed through several stages of formation, facilitated by various intercalary elements and events. Similarly to the way chemicals represent bonding agents between molecules and polymers, I have adopted Manuel De-Landa's 'intercalary element' approach to the function of a price mechanism within a late medieval market. The feedback of regulatory institutions which I represent as a cross (+) would go on to have a significant effect upon the development of complex meshworks of markets. For example hierarchies of meshworks and meshworks of hierarchies...

The interweaving of heterogeneous mineral meshworks within granite provide me with an analogy for networked markets. By dovetailing these conceptual models, a narrative is constructed, not only around deviancy and its relationship to socio-economic stable states, but of the cyclical, rather than linear processes which characterise these developments.

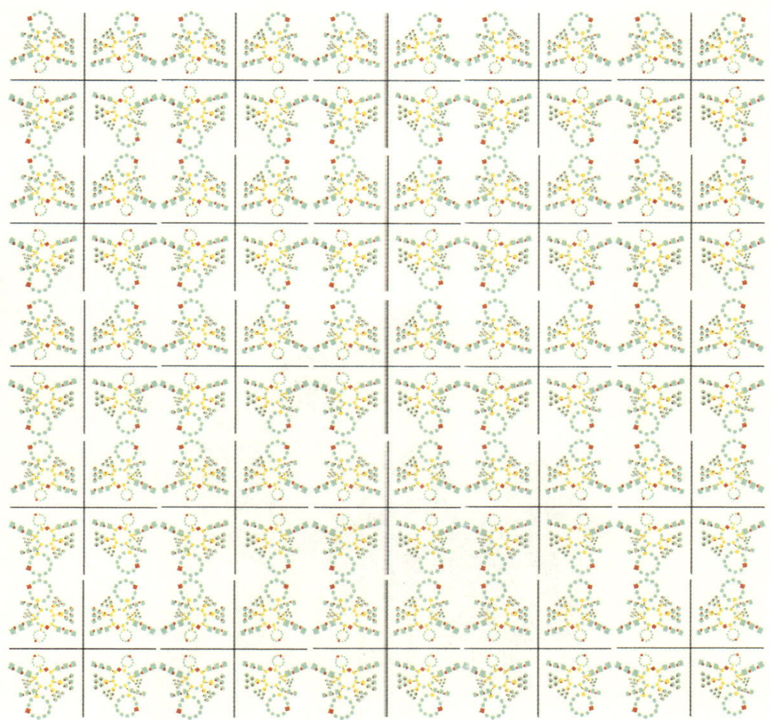

In this way one can begin to understand the scale of regulatory powers that were to sweep across the European continent as markets came to dominate flows of material and labour energy. Michel Foucault and others have documented the way in which stratified, hierarchical systems of organisation such as the 'house of correction' emerged as suprajudicial powers in France, Germany and the UK.

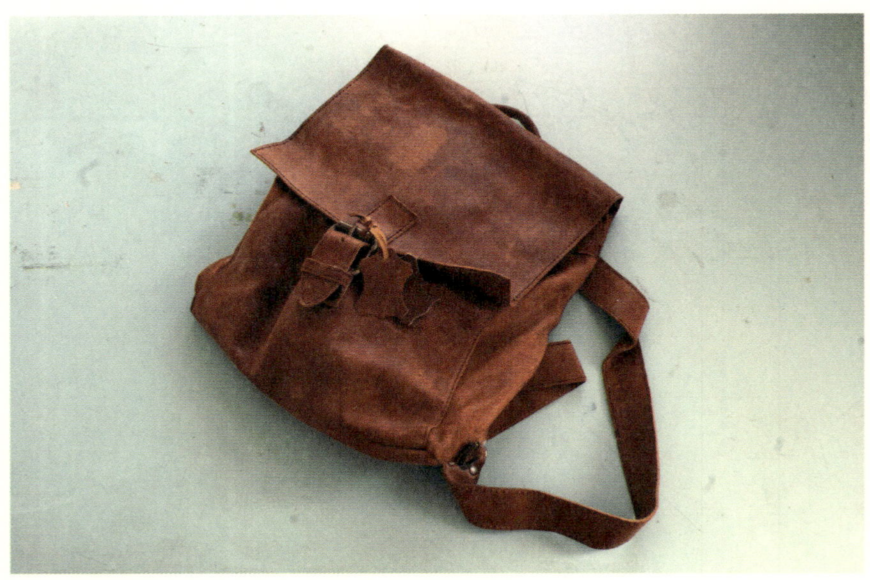

A contemporary leather satchel made in Hungary

A Nonlinear Market Model

Imagine traveling three days to acquire dressed leather with which to make a satchel. The leather can be manipulated into carrying tools of all shapes and sizes and I can charge a mark-up on the leather for my labour. Only, the journey to and from my leather supplier slows production and this adds to the overall cost of the enterprise. Once the techniques for dressing leather are mimicked, and vice versa, those in the business of dressing leather learn how to make satchels, a web of reproductive innovation drives expansion and competitive (re)production. In a sense, this autocatalytic process, one that continuously triggers a chain of reactions, creates new tools to be carried within the satchel and represents the birth of big business[7]. As satchel production (amidst innumerable other production techniques) advances, measures of regulation are set by access to materials, labour and opportunities for trade. As a simplistic example, the medieval satchel maker operated under the constraints determined by geological, economic and later, political circumstances. As an outlier producer, such a scenario would have been relatively precarious and many such small production centres fell under the wax and wane of late medieval trade routes, harvests and fluctuating prices[8]. To be more specific, as buyers at the nearest market diminish we can understand the economic environment as enacting a form of negative feedback upon the villagers producing leather products. This would regulate the amount of satchels being made and in turn the capacity at which the whole enterprise could realistically expand. Fundamentally, oils, beeswax, leather and labour are but the 'tip of the iceberg' of differentiated components or 'things' involved in these transmutations of energy, themselves regulated by the positive or negative feedback of a disbanded series of checks and balances.

The markets where satchels and sandals are sold, on the other hand, are a more precise example of the performance of negative feedback. The market, whether globalised or in the flesh, illustrates energy transfers in an explicit manner. The results of what constitute long production processes lie on market stall

7   Big business;
'…by the twelfth century, prices throughout Europe fluctuated in unison, and this is what above all characterises a self-regulating market economy. This collective oscillation, this massive rhythmical breathing …can now be captured through the use of nonlinear models…;
Manuel DeLanda, *A Thousand Years of Nonlinear History*, 1997 p 42

8   Prices;
Ibid. DeLanda p 39–42

tables; these are my 'things'. On the other hand, at a contemporary, global market, raw materials or stocks are represented by figures on a screen. We nostalgically imagine horses and carts tracing paths across a network of mud tracks and vast plains before arriving at market and its developing regulatory systems. Each market performs an act of transformation; energy pivots around an attractor, or price point, seeking to become converted into a new state… Under the heady influence of a systems-theory, drawn across space and time, I imagine one of the stalls as a time machine, exchanging leather satchels for donuts, merkins for gherkins or sneakers for heroin. I have attempted to illustrate the mechanics by which such a colourful tableau may be woven through my geological/market diagrams.

Within the example of the market, a price system performs the function of negative feedback, regulating, for a given time at least, supply and demand[9]. Markets, like any other example I could choose differ between innumerable factors. Yet they are coupled to the flow of goods and energy. As such, the analogy holds: the flow of energy affects processes of reorganisation, changes in the behaviour of energy or 'agents' and the redistribution of materials. In the satchel example, energy is 'liberated' from the hide of a cow and reorganised by the supply and demand encountered at the market. Of course in human terms, a market, particularly a late medieval one, contains a good deal more texture than the above diagrams are predisposed to reveal. My empirical research in the following chapter does go some way to adding a degree of socio-political texture to the overall argument. Another way to approach the complexity of this model is to begin to approach the nature of human relations, debated, forged and governed around the exchange of material goods and services. This task will be returned to in Chapter IV.

<u>A Short Introduction to the Emergence of
Regulatory Institutional Apparatus</u>
In order to establish secure methods of payment and rights of usage, institutional regulation and the enforcement of trade agreements had to be built into a market's organisational apparatus.

[From this point of view] cities arise from the flow of energy-matter, but once a town's mineral infrastructure has emerged, it reacts to those flows, creating a new set of constraints that either intensifies or inhibits them ...Needless to say, the walls, monumental buildings, streets, and houses of a town would make a rather weak set of constraints if they operated on their own, of course they do not. Our historical exploration of urban dynamics must therefore include an analysis of the institutions that inhabit cities, whether the bureaucracies that run them or the markets that animate them ...Markets and bureaucracies are, however, more than just collective mechanisms for the allocation of material and energetic resources. When people exchange goods in a medieval market, not only resources change hands but rights of ownership ...Hence, market transactions involved the presence of collective institutional norms (such as codes of conduct and enforceable contracts).

Manual DeLanda, *A Thousand Years of Nonlinear History*, 1997 p 29-31

9   Supply and demand;
'The market is a ferocious dictator, but no one person takes decisions. It just happens, or so it seems… The forces of supply and demand, we are told, act as signals. Nobody knows how much tin we all need at the moment. But if too little is being produced, the price will go up because of shortages. If the price goes up there is a super-profit to be made. And where there is a super-profit, there will be an inflow of capital. Capitalists making average or below average profits in other sectors of the economy will be attracted to tin production. To keep pumping the stuff out of the factory gate they will be prepared to hire more workers. They may even have to post higher wages, to attract workers from other industries. The system is unplanned. But the capital will keep on flowing in as long as there is money to be made. This is what Adam Smith called the "invisible hand" in celebrating market forces. As more capital flows in the price of tin will be beaten down and the rate of profit in that sector return to the average. Quite often capitalists will overshoot, respond to the shortage by overproducing, leading to unsold stocks and bankruptcies.'

Mick Brooks, *An introduction to Marx's Labour Theory of Value, In Defence of Marxism*, 2002, Part 1

This describes an aspect of negative feedback as it works to reproduce the stable conditions necessary for a market's and city's on-going survival. Additionally, the processes of negative feedback have impacted a much wider, political process of organisation. In vulgar Marxist terms, the economic evaluation and regulation of goods can be used to illustrate the estimation of an individual's worth against a scale of 'deviant' to 'desirable' as this mechanism performs within society at large. This is to say that, as the instrumentalisation of the human body-as-labour power becomes the defining relationship between the landed and manufacturing classes and their lower, proletarianised subordinates, an ideological apparatus developed, sometimes pulling, at other times simply reflecting these relations and attitudes to the labouring body. Part of this system of thought (reflected in Federici's quoting of Jean Bodin) is that the wealth of a nation amounted to the size of its population. Thus economic and biological (re)production was placed at the top of the scale of desirability within an emerging bourgeois sensibility.

Indeed Federici has traced such a sensibility toward the treatment of 'unproductive' women in the contemporary world:

> *But the 'battle to make wealth' is 'waged [above all] upon the mature female body' (Bonate 2 3: 1) because old women are believed to pose a special threat to the reproduction of their communities, by destroying crops, making young women barren, and by hoarding what they have. In other words, the battle is waged on women's bodies because women are seen as the main agents of resistance to the expansion of the cash economy, and as such as useless individuals, selfishly monopolizing resources that the youth could use. From this viewpoint, the present witch-hunts, no less than the ideology the World Bank promotes with regard to land, represent an inversion of the traditional conception of value creation, symbolized by the contempt the witch-hunters display for the bodies of older women, whom in Zambia they have at times derided as 'sterile vaginas.'*

Silvia Federici, *Witch-Hunting, Globalization, and Feminist Solidarity, Africa Today*, 2008

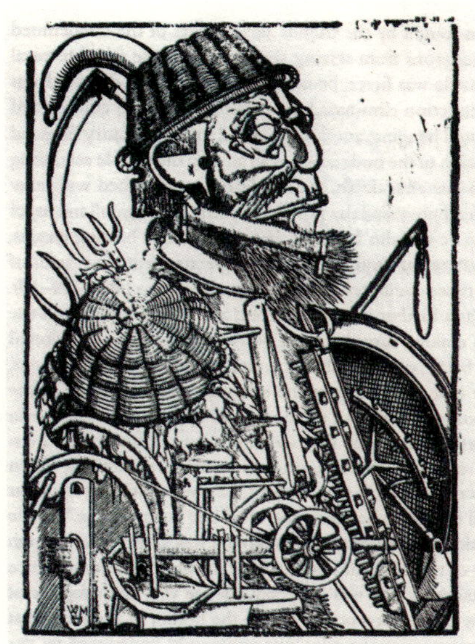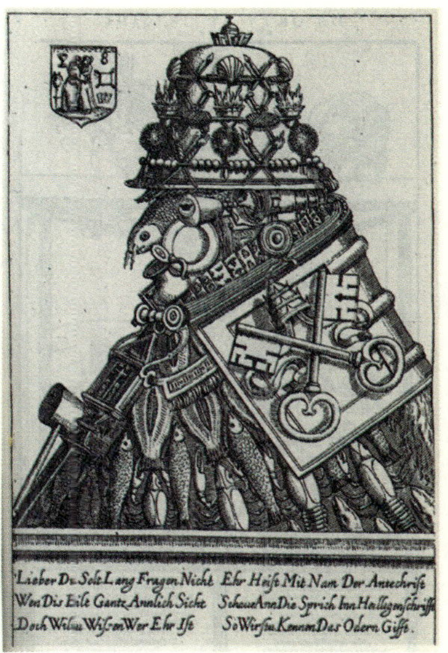

Sixteenth-century German engraving of a peasant represented as a collection of agricultural tools, left. Bust of the pope in the manner of Arcimbolodo, from a drawing by Thomas Stimer, Right. (Both images liscensed under the Creative Commons Attribution-NonCommercial 4.0 International Liscense, sourced from Silvia Federici, *Caliban and the Witch: Woman the Body and Primitive Accumulation*, 2004, and Luther Blisset, *Q*, 2003, respectively.

Though simplistic applications of market dynamics fall short of illustrating the complexity of either scenario, arguments in the service of female autonomy ask revealing questions: in whose interest and against which tide of change does the mature female struggle? Between these two periods, late medieval and contemporary, the female body is caught in the double bind of veneration and abstraction; ascribed the role of 'bearer of the divinity' and natural resource herself. As an institutional mechanism, women have at times been incorporated within systems of trade or, more precisely, honour. In medieval Ireland, so David Graeber tells us, disputes and trade often occurred in terms of honour and dignity, rather than material goods or currencies. When a lord or king acquired new dependents, such as slave women, his honour increased accordingly.

For Graeber,

> *Honour is a zero-sum game. A man's ability to protect the woman of his family is an essential part of that honour. Therefore forcing him to surrender a woman of his family to perform menial or degrading chores in another's household [such as laundry] is the ultimate blow to his honour. This, in turn makes it the ultimate reaffirmation of the honour of he who takes it away.*

David Graeber, *Debt, The First 5,000 Years*, 2011 p175

The institutions within which human economies come to reify bodies can be understood to instrumentalise acts of 'protection' or enclosure, not only of human units of exchange, but of the institution of indentured labour and trade itself. Female labour has been historically taken for granted. It follows, then, that under this patriarchal logic, female worth must be produced in some other way than their labour, particularly as either reproductive or honour value. Thus, the deviant label of 'mature' or 'unproductive' woman falls perilously outside of the cultural and institutional apparatuses that would otherwise limit the violence meted out against them in both medieval and contemporary times. A struggle for rights (e.g. workers right) is first and foremost a struggle for the terms upon which those rights are grounded (e.g. the right to be seen as a worker).

<u>A Meaningful Scale Parallax</u>
If we continue to assume that the behaviour of geological formation can be applied as a model for human interaction and organisation, as DeLanda does in *A Thousand Years*, then I would like to emphasise the distance to which I believe such an analogy can be taken.

The historical birthplace of markets lies outside of the purview of *A Thousand Years* which targets the years 1000-2000 AD.

However, markets, fuelled and facilitated by agriculture, trade and customs of exchange, constitute the standard anthropological identification of early Civilisation[10]. Thus, for this paper, they are important for the discussion of social organisation given the window markets afford us onto the role of negative feedback. But material analysis bears material limitations and I am inclined, perhaps disparagingly, to acknowledge the barriers that those engaged in the anthropological study of Ancient markets tend to encounter. Nonetheless, if it is accepted that groups first became banded around material goods and surpluses, might it not, by extension, also be possible to claim that societies are, at their core, the sum total of their energetic and material interactions? To do so would of course be an offensive oversimplification. Anthropological theses of ancient histories tend to be disproportionately grounded on material artefacts, in place of the spoken customs, laws and agreements which would have accompanied their usage and relative evaluation. If we are to leave the discussion of human consciousness to one side, it is necessary to question and frame the limits against which any (material) model can be applied to other fields of analysis.

Often, the material trace of complex human interactions converges on the oversimplified archaeological evidence of coins. To me the prime metaphor and substitute for human interaction is money. In relational terms, money is the ability to get work done. Despite and because of this strange, immaterial, substitutional dimension, the social analysis of money is complicated and intensely interesting! If I attempt to examine money as a type of regulatory institution or negative feedback loop, (within the price mechanism of a market, or as a means to service a social transaction such as a debt), we have to acknowledge the contingent value of money itself. The currency I hand to you as payment for the last space on a rescue helicopter isn't just money, or isn't just representational in its paper form, it is the formalised transaction that acts as the climax of a series of events and opportunities. On a more sober scale we can see that, as a resource, the value of money quickly disappears within a closed group or community, isolated from opportunities of usage. If we discuss the wider socio-political economy of a given banded group of inhabitants, our analysis is quickly vulnerable to becoming stretched beyond the tidy calculation of mathematical models.

> *The reasons why anthropologists haven't been able to come up with a simple, compelling story for the origins of money is because there's no reason to believe there could ever be one. Money was no more 'invented' than music or mathematics or jewellery. What we call 'money' isn't a 'thing' at all; it is a way of comparing things mathematically, as proportions: of saying that one of X is equivalent to six of Y. As such it's probably as old as human thought.*

David Graeber, *Debt, The First 5,000 Years*, 2011 p 52

Although money clearly plays an increasing role in the mechanics of markets, leading to the establishment of the money market as an institution of its own[11] in the 16th Century, what Graeber usefully highlights is the parallel, murkier world of subjective evaluation. Belief and trust, today crudely used to describe what money 'is', are present, though less palpable in every form of market organisation. Political economy is regulated not only by the theological or scientific models of the era, but also by the day-to-day exchanges, the minor fluctuations of life within the social proximity of others. That is to say, if the power of a system of social organisation, such as a market, can be harnessed through establishing regulatory practices, what substantiates the value of each regulatory code is the debate, meted out in the exchange of goods and services, around the appropriate nature of a given code of conduct. I have included this detail because dialogue, language and the spoken word are crucial to fleshing out the way in which new rules and regulations are extracted from and massaged or beaten back into a populous. Language, I will argue in Chapter IV, performs as an 'intercalary element' within the development of a social body of knowledge.

10   Civilisation;
John Reader, *Cities*, 2004 p 10

11   Institution of its own;
Manual DeLanda, *A Thousand Years of Nonlinear History*, 1997 p 32, 47

It's hard to imagine knowledge and information in the bounded terms that would have been prevalent in, for example, sixteenth-century France. The 'open-access' to information [12] characteristic of the twenty-first-century, gives us the impression that we are infinitely free to explore, compare, and contrast any potential worldview we choose. However, bound still within language, all this wonderful information may pale to insignificance should humanity discover, that due to a simple caveat, all our information is part of a corporate-state record (one that could indeed become attached to a global dictatorship) and that without freedom of communication between two or more persons what is possible will also be quite limited in material terms.

Intercalary elements are nodes or chemical events that are inserted between entities to facilitate an exchange of material or, often a catalysation that allows those two elements to consolidate into a new entity. In socio-historic terms, a drastic example of a linguistic 'intercalary' element would be the formalised law of 1606 that decreed all "beggars of Paris to be whipped in the public square, branded on the shoulder, shorn, and then driven from the city" [13], thus forcing the French population into a relationship with this law, regardless of their means of subsistence or gainful employment.

However, if a materialist philosophy situates events within material parameters such as labour, wealth and access to resources, it feels appropriate to use a practical scenario to explore my arguments. If the target of this paper is to ascertain the roles and characteristics of knowledge as deviancy, exhibiting a certain sympathy toward the ornery molecule, I should confess my desire to further such expressions within day to day life. In this chapter, I have been using models born from the study of thermodynamics and geology to schematise market dynamics. These are models that I will return to before locating my arguments within the history of the treatment of mental illness and the savage persecution of the witch hunt, in Chapter IV, if the reader wishes to skip ahead.

12   information;
Information must be understood in contrast to knowledge, which, in my opinion is only born from a certain intensity of experience, cognitive or otherwise.

13   City;
Michel Foucault, *Madness and Civilisation: The History of Insanity in the Age of Reason*, 1961 p 47

To review, this chapter has outlined i) stability and ii) zones of transition/transformation. My task now will be to tackle the emergence and role of deviations within these overall processes of feedback, in the following chapters. But if the reader will swerve with me, I will now draw upon empirical knowledge of a complementary opposite to orthodox market dynamics. It is my intention to use such knowledge to analyse deviancy in the next chapter. Here, I aim to flesh out some of the interactions between normative market dynamics in relation to agency and deviancy, and to elaborate on the production of knowledge in an environment of horizontality or non-regulation. Where deviation feeds back to create auto-catalytic loops and innovation in the above example of satchel making, the qualification and purpose of the deviant form I wish to explore in the coming chapter is more ambiguous, for reasons I shall explain. The work will have to further tackle the concept of agency, drawing on David Graeber and others while seeking to untangle exchanges of quality for quantity within the simulation of a human economy as socially engaged art practice.

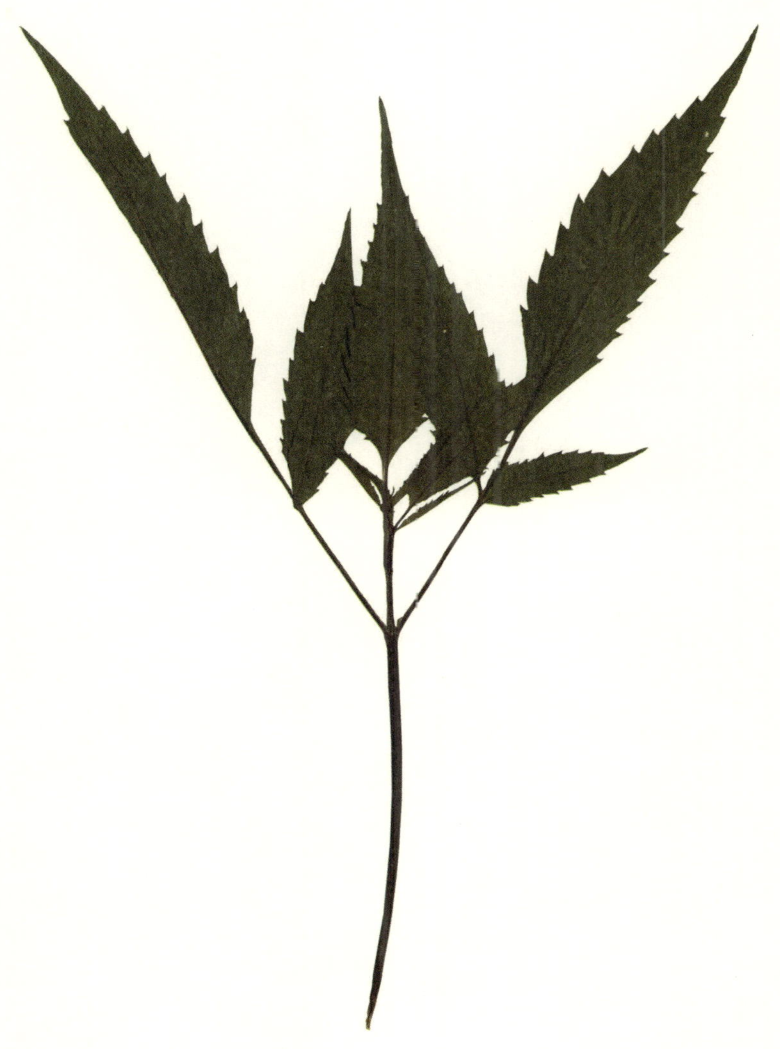

Debt & Guilt

Evaluation of *Time Bank* Project at the *Centre of Art and Urbanistics* (ZK/U), Berlin-Moabit

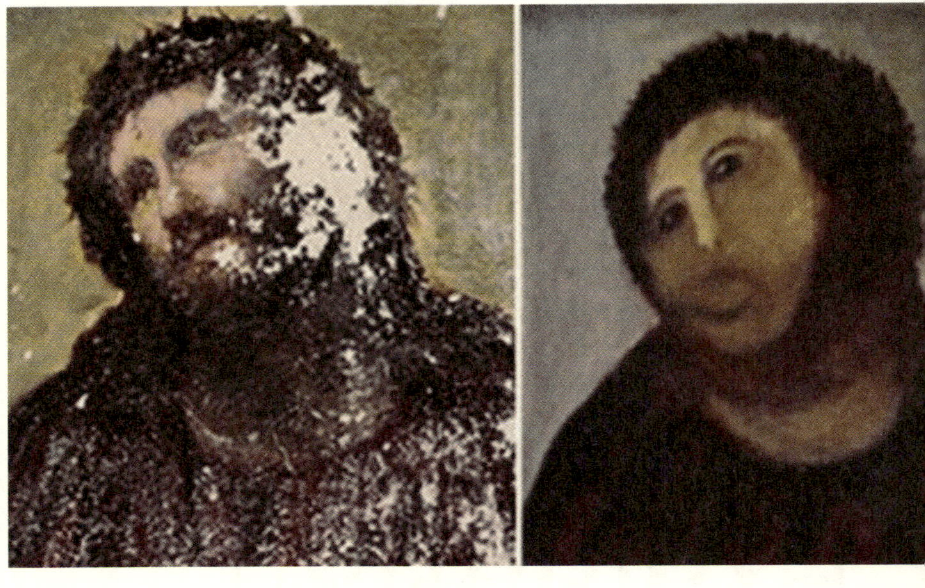

Left: Stephen Willats' concept of the artist as an agent to shifts in social behaviour in 1973.

Right: The contemporary attempts of corporations to tie this idea to their own public image.

Though it is too often assumed that artistic knowledge production is necessarily deviant knowledge production, artistic knowledge production can be understood as deviant, precisely because it doesn't attempt to produce anything…

<u>Background</u>
During a period of three years while living in London between 2008-2011, I worked closely with a group known as Transition Finsbury Park, itself working along the principles of the global Transition Town organisation. The goal of a Transition Town (TT) is to help facilitate the transition between a high to low carbon society. A pleasingly straightforward definition in words, I soon understood this to be an engagingly complex problem in practice. We screened films, hosted public presentations (one of which including a panel with the environmental advisor to Tony Blair, Michael Meacher

MP) and held D.I.Y demos in the Finsbury Park Mosque. By 2011, my work with Transition Finsbury Park (TFP) had culminated with a community wide festival that has since been adopted by new and additional groups in the areas of Manor House, Hackney and Finsbury Park.

One of the other key strategies of (the global) TT, in addition to the above PR campaigns, has been to establish gift economies or 'time banks' as a means to offset international importing and strengthen local bonds of co-dependency. A time bank is a form of skills exchange that allows users to swap their skills for time bank credits. These time credits may then be withdrawn from the wide range of skills available from the time bank group as a whole, say four hours worth of Spanish lessons or 12 hours of software programming.

The idea for a TFP time bank was highly popular amongst the steering committee which consisted, in true North London style, of campaigners, a representative from the local Mosque, the directors of an environmentally oriented photographic studio, a vicar and people engaged in the social welfare of the disabled and other vulnerable groups.

To my knowledge, the most successful time bank in London to date has been the one developed in Brixton. When the Brixton Pound was launched in 2009 it was an accepted currency for 80 local businesses and continues today. Up in North London, we never did get the loose ideas for a time bank network in Finsbury Park off the ground, though many of the local TFP initiatives have met with enthusiasm and support from local councils, three of which converge within the actual park of Finsbury Park (this detail creating something of a logistical nightmare when requesting permission to hold a public festival that would overlap on at least two different boroughs' turf).

However, the idea of a time bank remained, as they do all across the globe, an exciting prospect, not least because they would appear to offer, like all economies, answers to multiple dilemmas at a stroke. When I speak of dilemmas, I have to qualify the kinds of pressures that I face in day-to-day life. And I will try to do this by describing the distinction between what are for me an issue as opposed to a problem. The former (what I will call an issue, meaning an issue to be taken seriously enough to warrant action) are rather rare for Western Europeans such as myself. They would probably constitute, more often than not, a life threatening disease, severe domestic or other forms of abuse or perhaps finding oneself taken against one's will. There are, of course, additional dimensions to this but the point I'm trying to make is that, in short, Westerners face far more individuated problems than the kinds of societal breakdown that would necessitate an actually functioning 'time bank' such as warfare, infrastructural breakdown or natural and/or economic disasters.

Despite the inertia that attended to the TFP time bank idea, in 2014, my mind became set on setting one up in Berlin. Through conversations with the artist/researchers Matthias Einhoff, Miodrag Kuč, Pedro Victor Brandão and others, an idea began to take form. It was agreed that the project would be sited at a bi-weekly flea market at the Gütermarkt ZK/U at the Center for Art and Urbanistics Berlin-Moabit. At the peak of this engagement I was able to try out a further gambling-artwork wherein the time bank, known as ZEITBANK offered the public the chance to find an exchange of needs by playing a lottery. This was an experimental survey in action, known, simply, as the ZEITLOTTO.

Before I continue, it should be noted that the playful and experimental nature with which this project was approached should not detract from the social ills of alienation, time-poverty and the debt crisis that the Berlin-Moabit time banking project sought to address. Nor would I want to ignore the genuine investment everyone in the group made towards fostering discussion and seeking to deliver actual, material exchanges of skills and services. I would simply like to draw a distinction here between the theoretical platform the project established, mostly for a localised audience and participantship of players, and the immediate material concerns of those currently facing the thin edge of social welfare and security, for example in the refugee centres that continue to emerge in the project's focal area of Berlin-Moabit, in the following months and years.

Without becoming bogged down in metaphysics, the kinds of injustices or discomfort that lie within the realm of what a time bank at the Centre for Art and Urbanistics can serve to diminish are, in the end, limited to the gestural. If one reads the ZEITBANK as an exchange of knowledges (facilitated by a coupling of needs: a person requests gardening and offers baking, for example), there is a certain irony here: socio-cultural capital is something we all posses or have access to but that not everyone knows how to use. It consists of a set of customs, manners, references and often quite subtle expressions of class and cultural history. What the ZEITBANK proposed to do was demystify the way in which currencies and (by extension) markets work, and thereby make the public aware of capacities they already possessed.

The term 'cultural capital' has been described as the non-financial 'assets' used to further the individual within society. To understand how this is accrued we have to conceptualise the creation of cultural capital as an intersection with the production of meaning, value and affect in a very similar way to additional forms of 'immaterial labour'. Both cultural capital and immaterial labour react to and further subtle trends within cultural signification. In short, for artists like myself, cultural capital is 'the (art)work': that which translates a series of assertions and insights into experiential affect [1]. Maurizio

1   Affect;
'The artist's role [in the Creative Quarter], then, is to take part in what Hardt and Negri would term "affective labour": to work across the "social terrain" to produce "feelings" and "affects" that generate value for capital. Or we might call it "biopolitical production": they "produce" a lifeworld – a vibrant, cool, "happening" social terrain. In other words, they make a place seem "creative" by doing what they do – putting on shows in DIY spaces, organising talks, etc, etc...'
-David Bell, *Creativity, Capital and Commons in the Contemporary City*, 2013, Talk at the Centre for the Study of Social and Global Justice

Lazaratto has identified immaterial labour as the cognitive dimension inherent to new auto-managerial labour processes from the 1980's onwards.

[It is] the activity that produces the 'cultural content' of the commodity, immaterial labor involves a series of activities that are not normally recognized as 'work' - in other words, the kinds of activities involved in defining and fixing cultural and artistic standards, fashions, tastes, consumer norms, and, more strategically, public opinion.

Maurizio Lazaratto, *Immaterial Labor*, 1997

The cultural capital of the time bank lay within the cool, alternative, left-liberal politic of establishing one's own currency as an art project.

It performed as an attraction toward the Gütermarkt ZK/U (and ZK/U more broadly) with explicit references made by the public, who, in turn, through interviews and event tickets, became immersed within its overall development. The 'capital', here, is produced by the established cultural venue, the working group and the public themselves, all of whom are acting as producers and consumers at different levels and at different times. For instance, a director of the ZK/U buys a ZEITLOTTO ticket and is paired with a member of the public to swap car washing for sewing; the relationship with cultural authority is temporarily morphed, facilitated by the ZEITBANK group, but falls back into place once the transaction is enacted. In a sense, there is only an alternative relation between a director and a member of the public while the exchange is outstanding, while there is still a debt to be serviced. In explicit terms, the values accrued here are various but the final profiteers are the ZK/U; as with as any casino, the house always wins.

Socio-cultural capital can expire like any other form of currency once the guarantor defaults, leaving an incomplete puzzle and a debt. In this case, it is a debt of meaning that was ironically exchanged for content. Claire Bishop argues that one justification for the private or state support of socially engaged projects is its allocation as a means to service a breakdown in social coherence. She writes,

> *This injunction to activate [the audience] is pitched as a counter to false consciousness and as a realisation of the essence of art (or theatre) as real life. But the binary of active passive always ends up in deadlock ...high culture, as found in art galleries, tends to be produced for and on behalf of the ruling classes; by contrast, 'the people' (particularly the marginalised and excluded) can only be emancipated by direct inclusion in the production of a work. This argument underpins [New Labour] arts funding agendas influenced by policies of social inclusion. Its hidden assumption is that the middle classes have leisure to think, while the marginalised can only engage physically; this argument reinstates the class prejudice where working class activity is restricted to manual labour.*

Claire Bishop, *The Social Turn, Collaboration and Its Discontents*, Artforum International, 2006

Bishop establishes two forms of production here, cognitive and more physically immersive. She is also therefore highlighting two different modes of cultural reception born from the life experiences tied up with these forms of production. These clearly overlap, particularly in today's working world. But if we try to understand the ZEITLOTTO in the terms of both forms of labour and cultural reception, cognitive 'high culture' and more participatory, physical stimulation, nuanced aspects of the work come to light. If the project sought to demystify the workings of markets and currencies by simulating abstract money through a material, social form of currency, both forms of production, according to Bishop's dualistic reading of artistic audiences, were at play. Yes, we wanted to create a platform for all sorts of skills, all sorts of backgrounds and expectations of the artwork. If it was idealistic to do so, it was also a form of progressive utopianism, an aspect often lacking in the narrowly funded and organised operations of an art institution's cultural programming. Let us celebrate the pursuit of utopianism within the artwork, politicised through all the complexities of gendered, monetary and class contexts.

In broad terms, it would indeed seem that both state and private agencies have used arguments of corporate social responsibility to impact upon their public image, on the one hand, and the electorate, on the other (please see the art-favela referenced below as particularly disturbing conglomeration of this formula). One might then argue that if we can conceive of socio-cultural art projects like the ZEITBANK as servicing a social 'deficit', such a debt can only be passed on and deferred so many times, precisely because without a functioning time bank there was nothing really being exchanged! The mechanics of such a scenario are not new and they are not necessarily nefarious. But to work with the idea of a currency, with debt, culture and trust, organises these relationships in a way that may understandably leave a bad taste in the mouth. Eventually people want to know what you are doing with their data, their excitement and faith. As with so many aspects of the informal economy that serve to support and, let's face it, run the culture industry, this creates a nuanced environment that bears the responsibility of high expectations, requires scrupulous research and demands attentive timing. The following project description relates the efforts of the ZEITBANK in detail:

<u>An Attempt to Set up a Time Bank at the Centre of Art and Urbanistics (ZK/U), Berlin-Moabit</u>
Between 2014-2015 a working group operating under the collective title Schuldkrötensyndikat, sought to establish an economic exchange system for Berlin-Moabit entirely free from financial transactions. The working group consisted of Lia Bergaue, Jolanda Todt, Rafael Polo and myself. It is also important to mention the support and creativity of the d.i.y Church radio station who worked

closely with the group to air some of our work from Berlin. Our collective name (Schuldkrötensyndikat) derived from a double double play on words, across German and English. The German Schuld or Schulden means both debt and guilt depending on slight variations of usage. When the idea of the collective title Syndikat (in English, syndicate) was first suggested, I immediately thought of criminal underworlds that seemed to convey an overtly sinister image. It was pointed out, however, that the association between criminality and anarchic syndicalism was no coincidence. Indeed, a syndicate is simply a collective of groups that seek to promote a common interest. Today, my dictionary uses both financial and criminal organisation as explanatory examples.

Our first foray as a collective, following a series of interviews I made with those using the Gütermarkt ZK/U, was a lottery wherein (any)one could enter into the forthcoming ZEITBANK network. The lotto, named ZEITLOTTO, was to work in the following manner: a player made a request written directly onto the ticket, such as language lessons, car washing or whatever they needed. They then made an offer depending on which skill or service they wanted to offer as a means to buy themselves into the game. The game was presented as an opportunity to win other people's skills and time. The winners were announced live one week later on d.i.y Church radio that was also broadcast at Gütermarkt ZK/U itself.

Framed in the language of debt, our attempt to foster interest and participation within the time bank owes a lot to the work of left wing and Marixist thinkers like David Graeber, Maurizio Lazzarato, David Harvey and others. Of particular interest to us was Maurizio Lazzarato: a sociologist and philosopher living and working in Paris, where he studies immaterial labour, the breakdown of the wage system, and 'post-socialist' movements. Following the success of the ZEITLOTTO held over two events during Christmas 2014, I wrote the following manifesto under the collective name of the Schuldkrötersyndikat. Though never formally published, aspects of the manifesto were delivered to the public during the penultimate event at the Gütermarkt ZK/U in June of 2015.

Schuldkrötersyndikat
A Manifesto

The principal explanation for the strange sensation of living in a society without time, without possibility, without foreseeable rupture, is debt.

Maurizio Lazzarato, *The Making of Indebted Man,* 2011

Concept - The Schuldkrötersyndikat seeks alternatives to the time-poverty inherent to late capitalism. In employing seemingly contradictory ideas such as the formation of an autonomous-collective, we recognise that critique comes from care and that solitude can also be a form of solidarity. The Syndikat takes it's jump-off point from the double meaning of the German word Schuld (debt+guilt). Today our ability to make social connections is blocked by an undercurrent of debt+guilt to the global megalith of capital and to the next generation.

As Maurizio Lazzarato has observed, Schuld (DE), or debt, has come to replace time as the galvanising agent in the production of possible futures. Where paper money once operated as the symbolic exchange of trust - to pay the bearer the sum of ..., the investment in credit represents a fundamental restructuring of our relationship to the possible and to power. The neoliberal model of laissez faire capitalism requires new forms of controls. Therefore credit is offered as a means to control the future and therefore the present.

At its core, money is a fundamentally political tool and not one of commerce. Contrary to what may be supposed, monetary systems are not of commercial but political origin. Specifically, they were developed by central hierarchies to facilitate the extraction of agricultural surpluses and the raising of taxes [2].

As there is no means by which to objectively calculate the future capacity of the debtor to repay her/his debt, she/he is locked into the capitalist power relation as it stands today. Given the material impossibility for all debts on the books of national, private and individual interests to ever be paid, debt takes on the quality of a second translation from the German word Schuld or Schulden: guilt.

Faith, if you like, has been shifted away from the Western religions and spiritual practices to be heavily re-invested within the money form. The natural consequence of a capitalist system based in infinite growth (as long predicted by Marx), is the total abstraction of labour, collapse and misery for anyone unable to service the material impossibility inherent to the capitalist system.

What do we need? What do we want?

Reorganising, though never quite escaping normalised systems of socio-economic value, has been the pursuit of autonomist marxists for generations.

The Syndikat are suspicious of the contemporary fetish for online connectivity and self-surveillance. A typical Syndikat event will seek to discuss and broadcast both intellectual and practical concerns beginning with the needs and desires of the Syndikat itself, in public. There will therefore be a necessary element of philosophical, political and economic theory within our programme. The core aim of the project is to develop a set of social and political skills that may then be applied in other situations/localities while establishing a sustainable base at the ZK/U, Berlin-Moabit.

To summarise, we anticipate an exchange system for Berlin-Moabit that is entirely free from financial transactions: a time bank that serves the needs of the community in total. Our practice seeks to develop methods of artistic and social collaboration that advance a critical understanding of the democratic, non-exploitative reproduction of day-to-day life. The project is inherently sculptural in so far as the territorial occupation of space remains at the heart of social, artistic and political survival. If we are on the one hand engaged in establishing a theoretical territory with which to act, we are on the other establishing a space to speak from.

2 Taxes;
Manuel DeLanda, *A Thousand Years of Nonlinear History,* 1997 p 35

Thus, from late 2014 onwards, initial research was conducted by interviews at the Gütermarkt ZK/U. I recruited new members that helped to establish a sense of direction and trust before regretfully watching the project dissipate through a series of six events at the Gütermarkt.

Within the formulation of the time bank discussed here, known as ZEITBANK, the public relations of the project, which substantiates a lot what that project is, were very carefully planned, with an arc of activity drawn up over a two-year timespan. Holes appeared, not when energy ran out as such, so much as, when the necessary commitment to a consistent re-injection of enthusiasm

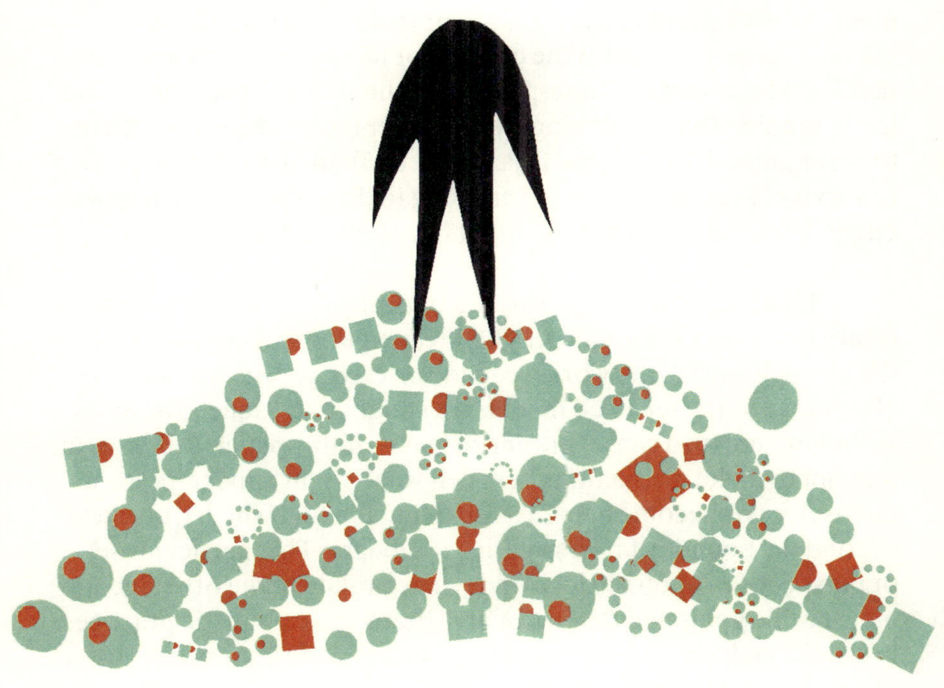

In the absence of the price mechanism and regulatory institutions our time banking experiment did not support a binding set of values. One might say that left wing ideals collided with the culture industry's inherent pragmatism.

became apparent, levels of commitment parallel to what I can only imagine is required when having a baby. The burden I set myself within the ZEITBANK project was disproportionate. To perform as a site of socio-economic political resistance and cultural hub all-in-one was simply incommensurable with the time, resources and personal commitment available in that instance. No matter how well intended any project is, without a surge of political, artistic or, frankly, financial inspiration, there was the sense that some of us felt constrained to move freely in other spheres. To do so would have been to ignore what I increasingly saw as an unserviceable commitment to the ZEITBANK, our emerging public, to art, and by proxy our 'reputation'.

A frustration at this dissolution can be explained away in terms of scale, ambition and practical commitment, but the virtue of having attempted such a hands-on critique of capitalist economy needn't only be reduced to a binary of failure and success. After all, if the project aimed at the critique of labour relations under a neoliberal economy of time-poverty, it should have been clear from the beginning that something would either have to be sacrificed (in time) or gained in (material financial terms), in order for the project to survive. Faith alone was never going to do it, though the way we engendered enthusiasm, you might have believed it would.

This lack of foresight was, then, a mistake. The value-added-return that I find within the ZEITBANK experiment depends on the extent to which the work we made offered a politically radical alternative to the received models we sought to critique. The analysis below, and (in a sense) the entire thesis of this paper, serves as an attempt to make distinctions between what might appear, present themselves or become named as deviant, and that which truly steps beyond the bounds of its normative forebears. This particular set of perspectives upon the idea of deviancy relate to the often incommensurable goals and desires of artistic and communistic practices.

Though it is too often assumed that artistic knowledge production is by pure association deviant knowledge production, this form of work can be understood as deviant, precisely because it doesn't attempt to produce items of value for an external system of evaluation such as fiat currency. This is explicitly the case in the artistic field operating outside of traditional gallery markets. Although, in the end, markets and culture always reabsorb subversion.

We have to recognise that there is nothing inherently humanitarian about the creative arts. Arguably, the pursuit of culture is always conservative in so far as practitioners are forever drawing on and reinforcing a canonised past. The idea and implementation of the artist as an instigator of changes in social cognition and behaviour (Stephen Willats, 1973), to which I refer above, inaugurated an unprecedented period of contact and radical practice(s) between artists and their public, a goal which I pride myself in attempting to continue.

That the artist has become so thoroughly instrumentalised within processes of socio-cultural value creation, corporate reputation laundering and being used to supplement the failing urban environment, begs for a new approach to the manner in which art and politics climb into bed. The banality of using the poor as aesthetic furniture demonstrated by Tadashi Kawamata and Christophe Scheidegger's Favela Cafe at Art Basel in 2014[3], only serves to illustrate the lax, confused or simply non existent politics that make art ideal for globalised luxury consumption. More strictly, social works are also in danger of falling short of the mark as either effective art or activism such as a remarkable exhibition I once saw when living in Florence, Italy. A group of photographers had the nerve to pay the city's homeless to be photographed (black and white), before exhibiting the mournfully lit images in a resplendent Medici-era apartment in the city centre for, 'invited guests'.

To enact an art project that derives its modus operandi from ideals based on autonomous social welfare, through gambling on a ZEITLOTTO, drives toward both the (non)functional capacity of the art object and its instrumentalisation as a means to deliver a

3   Favela Café;
Search for Tadashi Kawamata and Christophe Scheidegger's *Favela Cafe* on Vimeo.

socially just experience of equality. This didn't stop people playing the ZEITLOTTO or any other form of lotto that supports public arts programmes in Germany or the UK and that has clear winners and losers. I believe that what fascinated the Syndikat was the idea that a quasi-fictitious currency could somehow simulate the abstract values circulating within a flea market (at an arts centre), permitting them to be turned inside-out. This, in turn, proposed to reveal the meaninglessness of paper money and by extension the market economy itself. Rafael Polo insightfully positioned the Syndikat as the Gütermarkt ZK/U's complimentary and symbiotic opposite.

In hindsight, this was a project loaded with desire, ambition and expectation of an ideological magnitude. After all, we had a manifesto, a logotype, claimed political autonomy and were in the process of establishing a currency. For this reason, I would also come to believe that due to inflation (demand outstripping supply), our project (without currency) would soon become (ironically) bankrupt.

Discursive or engaged art and propaganda are concurrent cultural developments that gained significant traction from the mid-late twentieth-century onward[4]. The fact that love and money are essentially incommensurable means that establishing a trust-economy with a group of artist-cryptographers is inherently hilarious and awkward. A tension we explicitly brought to the fore by developing the time bank lottery, and the voluntary public submission of speech, movement and time in Lia Bergaue's Zeit-Bank in which the public were invited to waste their time for free. (These chimed with a tattoo gambling casino and other forms of tongue-in-cheek participatory practices involving gambling, developed over the previous eighteen months.) Thus, in this transitory way, subversive steps against normative self-exploitation were achieved by lending our audience the (socio-cultural) agency to become their own 'masters' during the ZEITBANK project. Yet by being asked to concurrently perform time-emancipation (authorised by the Syndikat), while playing along with the project, the audience were forced into a double bind: they became the masters of a self split into public submission to the whims of artists, in exchange for a fleeting moment of socio-cultural inclusion at ZK/U and socio-cultural emancipation from a normative free-market economy). Conflict between the differing expectations within the Syndikat and, perhaps, between the Syndikat and our audience, can be understood when we acknowledge that,

In a human economy, each person is unique and of incomparable value …because each person is a unique nexus of relations with others. [And that] the word 'human economy' is double edged. These are, after all, economies: that is systems of exchange in which qualities are reduced to quantities…

David Graeber, *Debt, The First 5,000 Years*, 2011 p 158, 9

It was simply not logistically possible to treat each player as a person of 'incomparable value', and each failure to do so impacted negatively upon the vibe of the overall pursuit. This is, I fear, just an inevitable part of what happens in the process of abstraction that a currency performs.

After months of postponement, we finally lost touch with the winners of the ZEITLOTTO who would no longer answer our calls. However, perhaps this is for the best, perhaps they will have a more textured expectation of politicised artistic practice (if they even read the whole affair as such), than simply providing amelioration for an absence of meaningful social exchange (historically linking capitalism to alienation).

I could suffer the reader to bear a lengthy, circular debate around the relative deviancy of one form of politicised art over another. But I'm less interested in answering to a final definition of deviancy (I do not believe one meaningfully exists), than establishing multiple, contextualised perspectives on the problem.

4   Twentieth-century onward;
As argued by Dan Graham in *The End of Liberalism*, 1981, sourced from the exhibition catalogue of Protest and Survive, Whitechapel Gallery, London, 2000

Each perspective aims to illuminate differentiated roles and behaviours that come to be named as deviant. These variants perform as coherent, if somewhat chaotic trajectories that course through the established and re-enforced norms that are inherent to the surrounding environment. Transgression expresses the vitality of that which is transgressed against. The norms' survivability depends also on its ability to adapt to accommodate new trajectories. (Or to regulate them through their negative feedback loops.) I am used to manners, norms and rules being flexible and many of us, particularly children, test their tolerances daily.

In the example of the ZEITLOTTO, I have demonstrated how chance, loyalty, and the essentially contingent nature of human relationships can be both acceptable, and offensive when illustrated through gambling with (a) social currency. The distinction between normal norms and the deviant or emergent norm becomes satisfyingly blurred within the artwork. Within the ZEITLOTTO, the distinction between the normal norm which states that gambling with peoples' trust is (clearly) awful[5] and a laissez faire 'free market' economy becomes subtle but palpable. This adds to the question of whether that which is truly deviant is even measurable in the same terms as that from which it deviates? (People and objects are noncommensurable!)

Surely, what we inherit as 'the deviant form' is actually the turgid fumes emitted as the real thing chuffs off into the distance; I increasingly believe that that which is truly transgressive does so against the very capacity for a thing to be known at all. This is another trait of deviant knowledge production that, in simple sociological terms, would constitute experiences related, but not limited to, subcultures and sects, graffiti, marginalia, drug use and almost all forms of carnal knowledge. These make up truths that cannot be acknowledged in their entirety, as to do so creates a faux pa that, once exposed, becomes impossible to ignore. This, in a sense, is all that sociological deviancy really is: it is just a matter of scale.

5   Awful:
Though we all know that chance is part of the human condition.

For example, the non-commensurability of people and objects is implicitly at the heart of society itself, though we know that under different (slave/working) conditions that is exactly how people have been and are treated. The actual capacity of humans to treat each other as objects only becomes deviant when it is brought to bear on those in one's local social environment, highlighting the potential for organisation and exchange: in other words, for marketing to spiral into every form of human endeavour. What we lack, due to nicety, is a language to approach this fact, hidden in the abstraction of capitalism itself. Art is primed for demonstrating this lack even if it is not appropriate as a means to develop the language in and of itself.

In the next chapter I will explore the conviction that psychological deviancy or madness is precisely the extent to which knowledge evades and therefore transgresses our capacity to qualify a thing at all. There, I will investigate the relationship between dialogue and reason as well as the role that dialogic exchange (the great trope of socially engaged practice) plays in the organisational apparatus of scaled-up medieval market societies.

ZEITLOTTO TICKET

Alex Head, Rafael Polo & Jolanda Todt
ZK/U GÜTERMARKT 14.12.2014

Mit ZEITLOTTO hast du die Möglichkeit die Fähigkeiten und die Zeit deiner Mitmenschen zu gewinnen. / ZEITLOTTO gives you the chance to win another person's skills and time.

ZEITLOTTO TICKET* / SCHEIN

Erstelle ein Gesuch – wie Sprachstunden, ein Glas Honig oder was immer du brauchst!
Make a request – such as language lessons, house cleaning, honey or what ever you need!

....

Mach ein Angebot – welche Fähigkeit, Produkt oder Dienst kannst du ZEITLOTTO anbieten?
Make an offer – what skill, product or service are you offering to buy your way into the game?

....

Name..   N° 0010203000025

Kontakt Number/Nummer...

Email...

*Dieser Lottoschein repräsentiert den materiellen Ausdruck einer abstrakten Idee, die in einem sozialen Umfeld realisiert werden will!
*This ticket represents the material expression of an abstract idea seeking realisation within a social body.

*This ticket represents the material expression of an abstract idea seeking realisation within a social body,
ZEITLOTTO Ticket, Dec 2014, designed by Jolanda Todt

Perverse Logos Expanding a web through the discussion of:

A Thousand Years of Nonlinear History, by Manuel DeLanda with *Madness and Civilisation: The History of Insanity in the Age of Reason,* by Michel Foucault and *Caliban and the Witch: Women, the Body and Primitive Accumulation,* by Silvia Federici

As stated at the beginning of Chapter II, the following endeavour forms the second part of a comparative reading between DeLanda and Foucault's works. However, in addition to these pieces I have included an analysis of the same period, from the activist-writer Silvia Federici.

The emergent manufacturing processes of the late renaissance and early classical era conditioned societies in new ways. These restrictions applied to time, liberty and the working person's proximity to the land. Due to the development of laws against the unemployed and the severe use of prisons, historians such as Michel Foucault have since named this period the 'age of confinement'. Given the legal and physical restrictions put in place to usher in a new area of obedient workers, one can describe this overall process as a consolidation of forms. Here, the male waged labour relation became consolidated at the expense of all other, prior labour relations. This much I will outline and source below. Manuel DeLanda has contrasted the large scale, stratified models that came to dominate European production processes in the run up to the Industrial Revolution, with the proliferation and survival of more traditional (horizontal) forms of manufacturing and crafts. I have chosen to focus on Foucault's study of the treatment of the mentally disabled as a way to analyse the era between the late medieval period, with the fall of the feudal power dynamic, and the early classical era.

I believe several aspects of these historical changes to social and political bodies within Europe cohere with a process of labour consolidation that necessarily extends into the behaviour, beliefs and thoughts of working subjects in addition to their possession of various manufacturing skills. As Karl Marx documented in *Capital, Vol. I,* the feudal labour relation was not dismantled easily or overnight and many peasants, or commoners, fought bitterly to protect the 'commons' they had come to view as their and nature's own.

In the great transition from feudal to capitalist Europe, however, both Foucault and DeLanda omit a crucial dimension to the wide processes of social engineering then underway. The destabilisation of peasant revolts, and the subsequent social, psychological and physical brutality unleashed upon those who questioned and challenged geographic and intellectual enclosure, could not have taken place without the mass execution of women as witches. This aspect of the so-called transition to capitalism is central to the power struggle of those that sought to reverse a top-down consolidation of agency and labour, enforced by new powers of the state, the church and mercenaries in the pay of the lords and royals. Due to this great omission, which we must first lay at the door of Karl Marx in his study of primitive accumulation, it is rarely mentioned that the so-called Age of Enlightenment was illuminated, in fact, by the burning pyres upon which lay the smouldering remains of countless female bodies [1]. After all, having been expelled from their land during the long demise of the feudal economic relation of serf and lord, expropriated peasants and artisans did not peacefully agree to work for a wage. More often, they became beggars, vagabonds

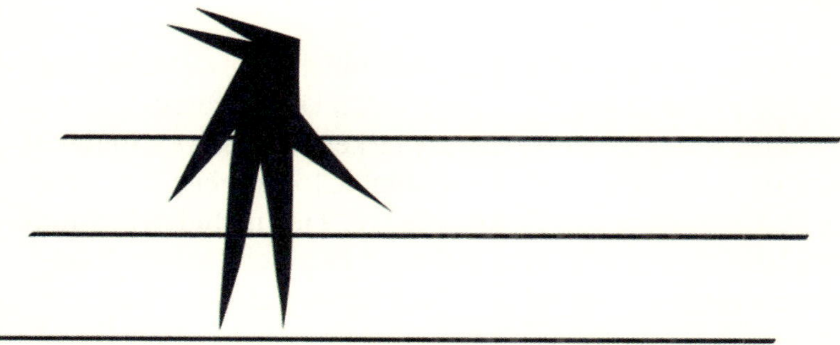

Following the fall of the Roman Empire in Europe, plots of arable land were handed down from generation to generation. During this period, known as the 'dark ages', many folk expressed a sense of autonomy and ownership over the land they tilled.

1   Female bodies;
'Though controversy concerning the size of the witch-hunt continues, regional estimates have been provided by Midelfort and Larner. Midelfort (1972) has found that in Southwestern Germany at least 3,200 witches were burned just between 1560 and 1670, a period when "they no longer burnt one or two witches, they burned twenties and hundreds (Lea 1922: 549).'
Silvia Federici, *Caliban and the Witch: Woman the Body and Primitive Accumulation*, 2004 p 208

or criminals. A long process was required to produce a disciplined work force. In the sixteenth and seventeenth-centuries, the hatred for wage-labour was so intense that many proletarians preferred to risk the gallows, rather than submit to the new conditions of work [2].

An explicit dimension to the persecution of witches and those practicing magic in relation to social class, as identified by Silvia Federici, is that 'high magic' was left well clear of the persecutions, as astrology and astronomy were considered aspects of the new scientific era[3].

In order to break apart the power base of the traditions that constituted the emergent European proletariat, a series of blows were struck to the lower-class body and mind political. Techniques of community destruction and destabilisation, necessary to create a subservient workforce, both abroad and within Europe, permit a characterisation of this period, further detailed below, as a series of violent lessons sanctioned by the emergent state, as a means to instil subservient behaviour to individualised labourers.

Women had the most to lose from the threats this new deal posed to their sites of social and intellectual reproduction. Driven from working the fields and at local markets, new laws stipulated the forms of work, now no longer available to women, thereby excluding and atomising female knowledge. This included techniques of contraception, one of the central ways in which women maintained a sovereign command over their bodies as more than vessels of reproduction. Equally, as women had previously laboured in both the fields, markets and in the home, as community builders and providers of child rearing, they constituted the front line of the class war that continued long into the late medieval and renaissance era.

These, highly obscured components to the background against which Marx and Foucault depict the parallel histories of

2   Work;
Christopher Hill, *Change and Continuity in seventeenth-century England*, 1975 p 219-39

3   Scientifc era;
Silvia Federici, *Caliban and the Witch: Woman, the Body and Primitive Accumulation*, 2004 p 1

'primitive accumulation' and the 'age of confinement', serve to enhance our understanding of the true measure of the oppression that people, and particularly women, were subjected to during this apparent morphological process of socio-economic consolidation. If the official, patriarchal rule of law is that which survived the violence symptomatic of the age, we can see, too, why the historical narrative of women's repression could not be carried through to the official account of man's 'progress' into the next era. This blind historicisation can only be expected from a white, male political elite (to whom both Marx and Foucault owe their privileged positions as intellectual thinkers), it is however, a shame upon those who would labour their lives through in the apparent critique of (white European) hegemonic power.

In counter-resistance to the female rejection of their own enclosure to the task of reproducing workers, the great witch hunt gained momentum. Ravaging communities and the fundamental trust between men and women, this scourge of legislated hatred would sweep through villages and towns alike until, at the end of the eighteenth-century bourgeois women themselves became accused in the climax of a process of social engineering that had by then fulfilled its core goals[4].

4   Goals;

Ibid. Federici, p 205

The Age of Enlightenment

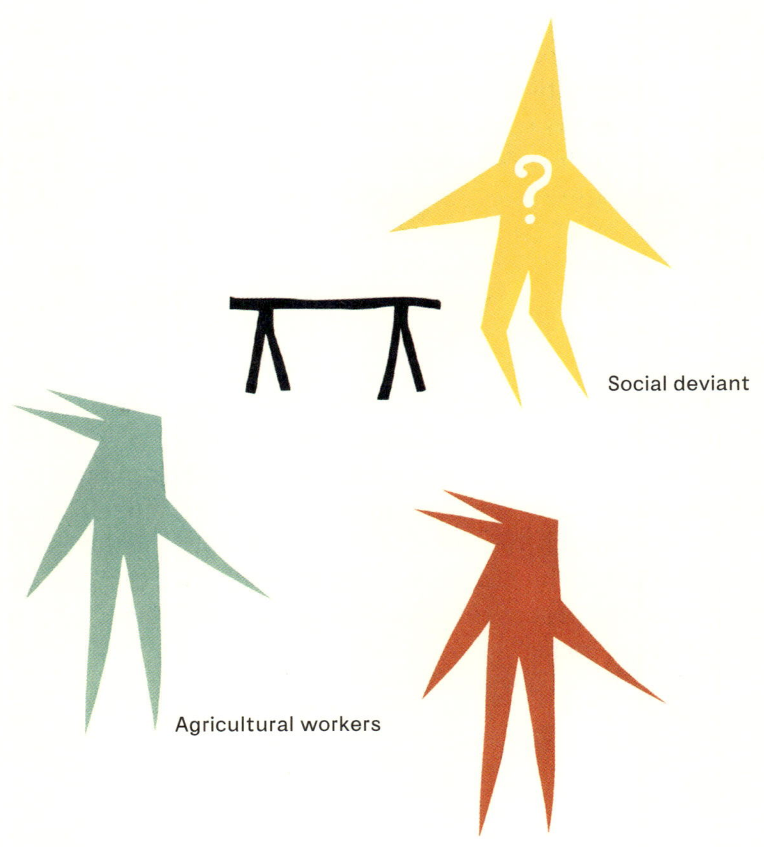

Much of the collective knowledge coupled to agricultural life became labelled as irrational, criminal and deviant during the age of enlightenment. For woman, farming the land and selling produce at markets provided two important sites for the exchange of knowledge.

Medicines and contraceptives featured among the ameliorative properties of herb gardens that were crucial to female autonomy. Autonomous contraceptive techniques allowed women to decide when and with whom they would reproduce and thus structure their lives more precisely.

Once agricultural workers were torn from the land during the mass privatisation of Europe (between 1450 – 1500), many formed roaming, rebellious groups. Women were primary targets in the breaking up of working people's strength and resistance to wage labour. After all, women had a great deal to loose, having nurtured the families and communities on which so many depended.

Vast disciplinary systems emerged in order to quell rural and increasingly urban unrest. Disciplinary violence such as torture and public execution have existed since the early days of civilisation but the degree of brutality was particularly harsh in medieval Europe. Collaboration between the church, an emerging state and Europe's royals ensured that the butchery historically associated with the medieval period was both rationalised and systematised during 'enlightenment'.

It is rarely mentioned that the so-called Age of Enlightenment was illuminated, in fact, by the burning pyres upon which lay the smouldering remains of countless female bodies.

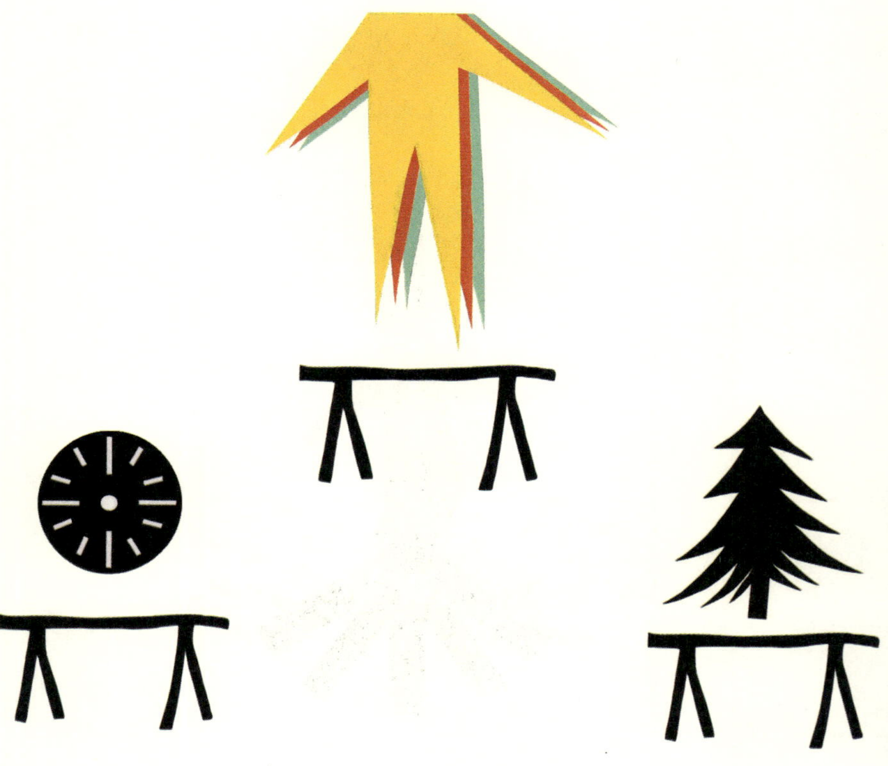

Naturally a heterogeneity of skills and belief systems continues to multiply across Europe and the world of global capital more broadly. Yet physchologically, and legally, the labour force had suffered a huge blow to its collective agency. Waged labour became the dominant organising principle while 'nature' underwent enclosure.

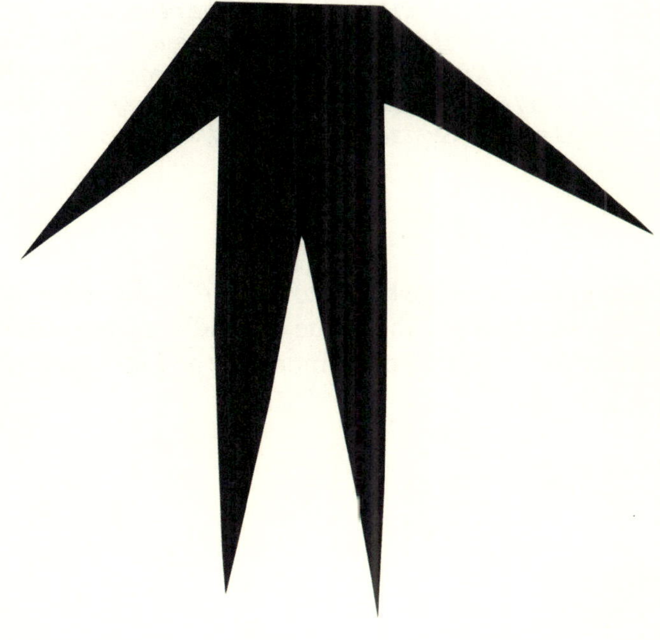

I have chosen to represent this condition as a headless figure. In my mind this corresponds both to the loss of historical connectivity with struggles for land, liberty and gender equality. Further, the headless figure also speaks to the public beheadings these crimes necessetated in the eyes of an emerging bourgeous capitalist state.

Federici demonstrates, by acute use of the public record, a broad articulation (we may read: sorting mechanism associated with negative feedback), of an ordering process through which the delineation of reason and unreason, (of scientific versus homeopathic medicine, for example), takes hold to ring in the very first coordinated, European wide socio-political stable state:

> *Thus, it is no exaggeration to claim that the witch hunt was the first unifying terrain in the politics of the new European terrain of the nation states, the first example, after the schism brought about by the Reformation, of a European unification. For, crossing all boundaries the witch hunt spread from France to Italy, to Germany, Switzerland, England, Scotland, and Sweden.*

Ibid. Federici, 169

Further evidence of the bourgeois desire to delimit women to the role of reproduction and the virtue of childbirth, are written into the severe criminalisation of infant mortality and infanticide[5].

5   Infanticide;
Ibid. Federici, p 88

The concomitant development of a population crisis, an expansion-
ist population theory, and the introduction of policies promoting
population growth has been well documented. By the mid sixteenth-century the idea that the number of citizens determines a nations' wealth had become something of a social axiom. 'In my view',
wrote the French political thinker and demonologist Jean Bodin,
'one should never be afraid of having too many subjects or too many
citizens, for the strength of the commonwealth consists in men.'

Jean Bodin, *Commonwealth*, Book II, sixteenth-century, quoted by Silvia Federici, p 87

Therefore, as we now launch into a reading of one male author
through the methodological apparatus of another, we would do well
to remember that the sociological idea of a moral panic followed by
a 'witch hunt' is rooted in a very real set of persecutions. And that
these persecutions continue today in the primitive accumulation
triggered by the endeavours of the IMF in places such as Northern
Transvaal, Kenya, Nigeria and Cameroon in the wake of an ex-
ported colonial European ethnographic of the very concept of devil
worshipping[6]. Closer to home, contemporary academic circles
must also acknowledge the shortcomings of the received wisdom
on the disciplining of the body, in that Silvia Federici has identified,

> *...Michel Foucault's analysis of the power techniques and
> discipline to which the body has been subjected has ignored the
> process of reproduction, has collapsed male and female histo-
> ries into an undifferentiated whole, and has been so disinter-
> ested in the 'disciplining' of women that it never mentions one
> of the most monstrous attacks on the body perpetrated in the
> modern era: the witch hunt.*

Ibid. Federici, Preface, 8

The absence of this dimension to Foucault's analysis of physical repression highlights how deeply forgotten female and other marginalized histories have become.

6   Worshipping;
Ibid. Federici, p 221

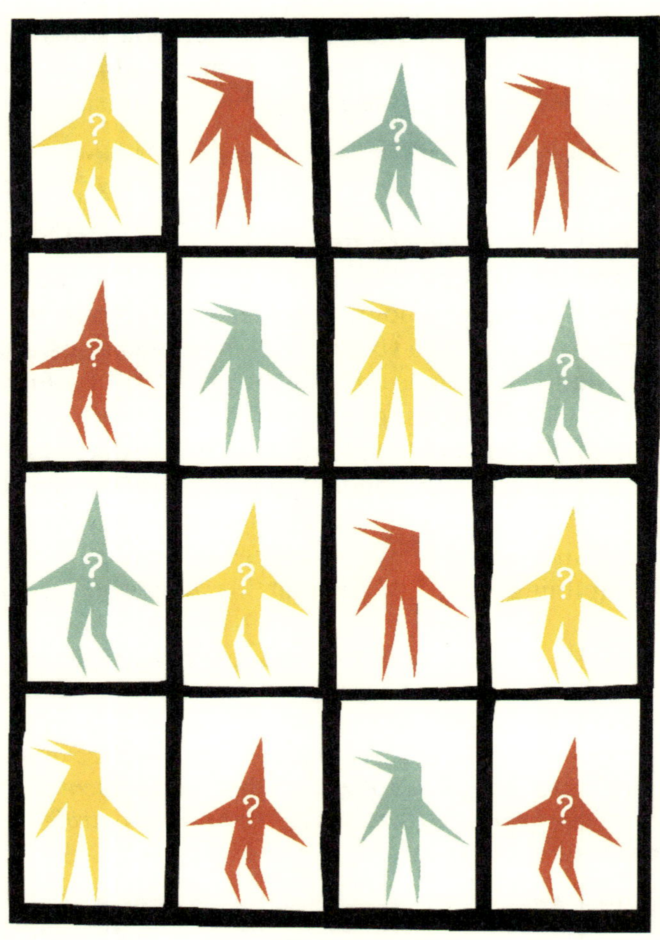

'In a hundred and fifty years, confinement had become the abusive amalgam of heterogeneous elements.'

Michel Foucault, *Madness and Civilisation – The History of Insanity in the Age of Reason*, 1964 p 45

Ibid. Federici, 197

Engaging a Scale Parallax

Within this paper I have made references to the experience
of a scale parallax; a kind of vertigo achieved by an author when
insufficient intellectual lubricant is applied in scaling up or down
between material. Such events can also follow when researching,
viewing, or simply embracing the 'other'; when new material causes
a gestalt; the shock of revelation or rude awakening. Though this
can be an unpleasant, disorienting experience, there are always
cases in which avoiding it is not an option. I cannot simply go for a
class of water, for fear of loosing my concentration on the subject;
the parallax is also trying to tell me something, to reveal something.
The feeling of spinning from over-intoxication, so it is said, is the
mind being forced to acknowledge what the body already gracefully
accepts, namely, that we are moving with the earth's rotation at 0.5
kilometres per second, itself in orbit around the sun.

To review the thermodynamic model outlined in chapter one:
homogeneous molar, chemical and social agents or entities can be

demonstrated to emerge from chaotic, heterogeneous systems and vice versa. Scientists and philosophers have observed patterns of behaviour whereby these entities seek out and form stable formations in a cyclical pattern throughout natural and social phenomena. In decomposition, lies the seed of yet a further stable form. Within the thermodynamic example of water boiling, this shift can be described by the increased movement of water particles as they are introduced to a sufficient source of heat. Increased movement on the molar level is measured by statistical mathematics as an increase in the possible behavioural forms or traits that a water molecule can display. The number of positions the water molecule can occupy increases rapidly as the overall thermodynamic system increases in heat. This is known as 'chaos' or 'disorder' in the scientific language of physics.

At the point of each bifurcation between one stable state and another (that is to say, at the point of transition where water molecules begin turning into a gas) lies a morphological arena. As DeLanda has argued, there are virtues to making analogous arguments with social and historic phenomena insofar as these models allow us to transcend a linear view of historic processes. To sympathise with a teleological, linear conception of history is, in this view, to ignore larger, cyclical processes of global and cosmic transformation as nature and humanity strive toward apparent progress. One way to understand nonlinearity is through the natural sciences.

Clearly, for DeLanda nonlinearity also offers a meaningful critique of capitalist labour relations. Insofar as a critique of the accepted notion of human progress is really a critique of the scientific, technological and moral 'progress' historically bound up with the

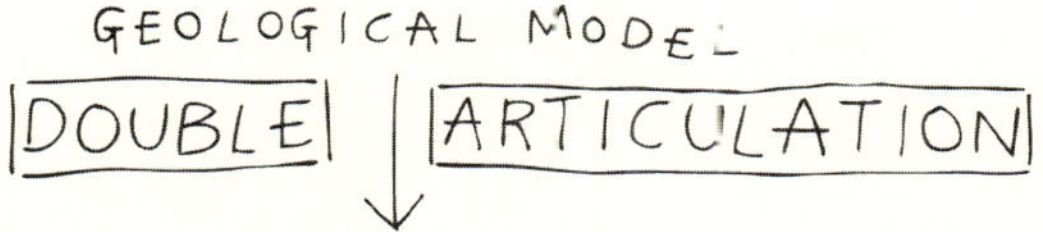

1. SORTING:
ROCKS CARRIED BY RIVERFLOWS
TO THE SEABED (EFFECTED BY
NON-LINEAR VARIABLES SUCH
AS PEBBLE SIZE + FLOW
PROPERTIES + RIVER BED COMPOSITION

2. CONSOLIDATION:

HETEROGENEOUSLY SORTED
PEBBLES ARE TRANSFORMED
BY SOLITIONS WITHIN WATER THAT
PENETRATE THE PORES BETWEEN

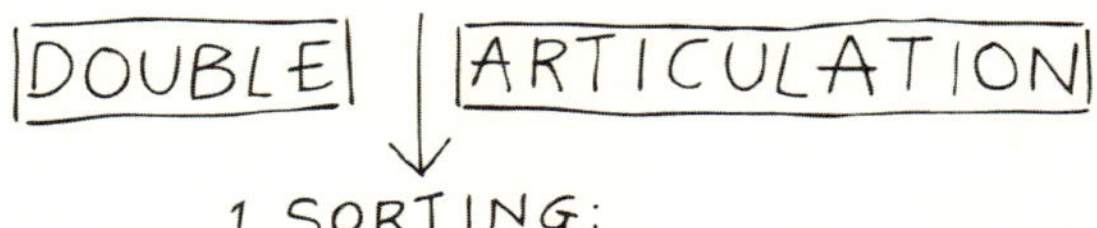

EVOLUTIONARY MODEL
DOUBLE ARTICULATION
1. SORTING:
GENETIC MATERIALS WITH ATTENDANT BEHAVIOURAL + PHYSICAL TRAITS BUILD UP WITHIN A GROUP OF THE POPULOUS
REPRODUCTIVE ISOLATION
A GIVEN SUBSET OF THE POPULATION IS MECHANICALLY OR GENETICALLY UNABLE TO MATE WITH THE REST
WHICH MEANS
2. CONSOLIDATION:
ACCUMULATED ADAPTATIONS ARE FORGED INTO NEW SPECIES PREVENTING DEVOLUTION ALL THE WAY BACK TO UNI-CELLULAR ORGANISMS

SOCIAL MODEL

|DOUBLE| |ARTICULATION|

↓

1. SORTING:

THOSE WHO HAVE GAINED PRIVILEDGED ACCESS TO CERTAIN ROLES FIND WAYS TO REPRODUCE THOSE CONDITIONS

|CRITERIA| |EMERGE|

↓

WITHIN THESE DOMINANT GROUPS FOR THE SORTING OF SOCIETY INTO CRYSTALIZED STRUCTURES

↓

2. CONSOLIDATION:

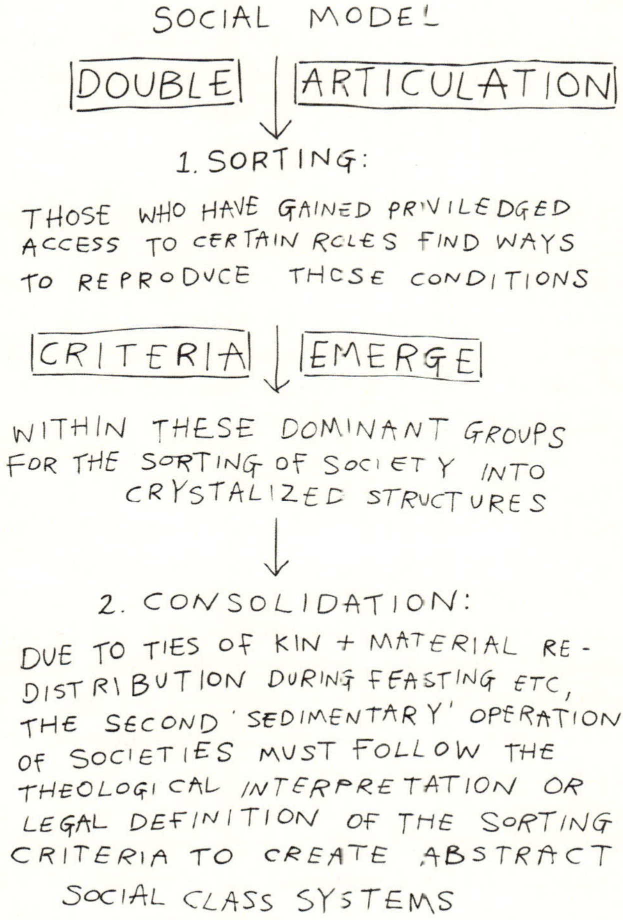

DUE TO TIES OF KIN + MATERIAL RE-DISTRIBUTION DURING FEASTING ETC, THE SECOND 'SEDIMENTARY' OPERATION OF SOCIETIES MUST FOLLOW THE THEOLOGICAL INTERPRETATION OR LEGAL DEFINITION OF THE SORTING CRITERIA TO CREATE ABSTRACT SOCIAL CLASS SYSTEMS hyperacceleration of capitalist systems of organisation. Nonlinearity performs as a critique within DeLanda's analysis of the latter half of the millennium addressed in his work A Thousand Years, because the development of capitalism was not the only possible response to the crisis of feudal power. Throughout Europe, vast communalistic social movements and rebellions against feudalism had offered the promise of a new egalitarian society built of social equality and cooperation. However, by 1525 their most powerful expression, the 'peasant war', was crushed[7].

To drive at nonlinear histories is but one means of exposing the concept of Western civilisation as a series of one-sided accounts that necessarily ignore the human and environmental cost of development. Humans, in their fear, typically conceptualise history in linear terms just as they conceptualize their lives in a linear, terminal fashion. When we reach deeper into the human mind, and into historical records, it becomes easier to conceive of a great wellspring of human endeavour, waxing and waning with the cosmos as a whole. Precisely this type of cosmic or astrological thinking has been deemed the erroneous magic of insubordination and insurrection, since it was recognised amongst slaves by the ruling classes of the late Roman Empire[8]. My contemporary heresy might consist of continuing to question the magic of money itself, but the material limits of the planet, abstracted through the discipline of economics, nonetheless suggest a larger cycle of planetary and molecular development: one that contextualises the human scale within a nonlinear cycle of creation and destruction.

In turn, I have argued that a nonlinear outlook situates the behaviour exhibited during a borderline state of transition, as part of a natural deviation of matter within on-going processes of negative feedback. The harnessing of such deviations can be modelled as a series of state interventions to secure stable power bases through political and economic systems,

7   Crushed;

Ibid. Federici p 61, (*The Accumulation of Labour and the Degradation of Women: Constructing 'Difference' in the 'Transition to Capitalism', Part 1: Introduction*)

8   Roman Empire;

Ibid. Federici, p 209

and other phenomena such as the creation of new artistic knowledge.

Processes of negative feedback can be applied from the study
of thermodynamic systems in an analogous way to historical and
social trajectories (see the geological/market diagrams). Societies
will often perform constraints on the individual in order to maintain
the basic conditions deemed necessary for its overall survival. The
extent to which such constraints are employed to further socio-
economic equilibrium, as opposed to furthering hegemonic power
and ensuring surplus extraction, is a matter of political and economic debate. Certainly in the stratified model of social hierarchy
elaborated by DeLanda, socio-economic stability is the prerequisite
and priority for a ruling group that wishes to maintain its position
of privilege. For DeLanda, schooling systems, institutions of law
or monarchical hierarchies simply represent the calcified form of
a process by which sorting criteria (one might read: negative feedback) are developed by an elite, and used to organise social actors
into the appropriate camps, in turn maintaining a stable state of
dominance referenced within the diagrams on the following pages.
As such, we could read the emergence of new forms, acting in deviant relation to a given, stable state, as transgressive to this mechanism of division and categorisation. Clearly, some social deviations
have historically been met with violent oppression, policed governance and repressive legislation.

The history of the treatment of mental illness, in particular,
describes an instance of heterogeneous groups that were violently
packed into homogeneous cells. What can be witnessed here are
inappropriate treatments shifting, under the weight of their own
demonic momentum, into institutionalised savagery as they enact a
large unwieldy process of rationalisation and social engineering.

In *A Thousand Years*, DeLanda found that where stability is
the desired trajectory within a space of market exchange (both as

the sum of multiple, coexisting traders within the price mechanism, and as a set of external trading regulations), a nonlinear course of events can be observed through negative feedback.

These nonlinear courses of events are characteristic of the entry point for Foucault's study of the treatment of the mentally disabled, in *Madness and Civilisation*, as well as Federici's study of slaves and female transgressors in *Caliban and the Witch*. Foucault's treatment highlights that which often begins as a heterogeneous combination of elements within the self-regulating dynamics of early markets as it becomes subsumed and homogenised within a cycle of greater and greater bureaucratic institutionalisation.

> *In several years an entire network [of workhouses] has spread across Europe. ...the same walls could contain those condemned by common law, young men who disturbed their families' peace, or who squandered their goods, people without profession, and the insane.*
>
> Michel Foucault, *Madness and Civilisation: The History of Insanity in the Age of Reason*, 1961 p 45

Foucault describes a coalescence of inmates, who would have received very different punishments in the previous centuries, or else none at all. Furthermore, DeLanda argues that although the current trend of our species is towards increasingly hierarchical forms of organisational control, this trend is itself constituted of both heterogeneous and homogeneous elements (and forms of behaviour) occurring within a far larger cycle of material and cultural transformation. The categorisation and division of elements into groups can be demonstrated to occur throughout multiple examples within European Colonial expansion. Within this period the form of deviance madness demonstrated was as much about one's capacity or willingness to perform economically as any sense of theological, scientific or moral standards used to explain away these groups' treatment. With Foucault's ambitious historicisation that links the social climate of the European seventeenth-century, shifts in

manufacturing and the violent oppression of economically marginal groups, the reader must also ask themselves whether human
nature is inherently cruel, or shaped into violence by a struggle for
survival.

Foucault draws reference to those who, once interned in a
workhouse and made to contribute their labour in exchange for
their upkeep, would later find it difficult to engage with group tasks
and meals outside of the workhouse. It is also not immaterial that
'madmen' were included in the proscription of idleness. Those
suffering from severe forms of mental disability such as paranoia
or schizophrenia would naturally have trouble working in groups.
From its origin, they would have their place beside the poor, '…In
the workshops they distinguished themselves by their inability to
work and follow the rhythms of collective life…'

Ibid. Foucault, p 57-8

Thus, as these persons represented zero potential for economic production, their fate became the whim of their jailor.
Without sufficient medical means for discerning the appropriate-
ness of one form of treatment (socialised or solitary for example),
large numbers of socio-economic deviants were, literally, grouped
together in mass prisons: 'in a hundred and fifty years, confinement had become the abusive amalgam of heterogeneous elements.'

Ibid. Foucault, p 45

As the story of mental disability and the persecution of
women as witches show, the regulation of unwanted forms of
behaviour, thought and self-sufficiency have also been interwoven
within the ways in which we discern power structures in relation
to the visible for centuries. Thus, the analysis of deviancy through
Foucault's *Madness and Civilisation* and Federici's *Caliban and the
Witch* provide this thesis a means to unite ideas around the cultural
production of (inspired, mad or scientific) novelty, power and

thermodynamics in a confluent manner. In this sense, the continued production of new knowledge around discrete aspects of modern history substantiates the great contributions of Michel Foucault and Silvia Federici to the history of ideas.

Perverse Logos

As an event within knowledge production, scale parallaxes are necessarily engaged with, avoided and/or navigated. What I am calling a *scale parallax* could also be called 'pushing the envelope'. Here, the envelope represents a field or discipline and the contents of the envelope are the sum total of knowledge pertaining to that field.

As the wisdom and techniques of one era pass into or dissipate at the emergence of the next, scientific analysis must also turn to speculative enquiry for guidance. What I once saw cannot again be seen from another pair of eyes; knowledge is subject to change. If the history of ancient mythologies is indeed an analogous history of human consciousness as the mystery schools teach, then some truth must attend to the suggestion that in five hundred thousand years time, what you have thought will be forgotten, but that you have thought will not.

> *...it is the common, if not universal human experience, that if we try to work out what is the right thing to do with our lives using all of our intelligence, if we work at it with a good and whole heart, if we exercise patience and humility, we can - just - discern the right thing to do. And once we have made the right decision, the chosen course of action will probably require all the willpower we are capable of, perhaps for just as long as we are able to bear it, if we are to complete it successfully. This is right at the core of what it means to experience life as a human being.*

So it is with madness and other aspects of the human condition that we fail to incorporate into the narrow scope of what passes for 'truth' within a given period of human history. The shift or cognitive lurch I am referring to, can be located within the heady speculation around mental illness within the classical period in its estimation of the condition of vertigo as 'insanity'. The unfortunate sufferer would have been deemed mentally ill, that is the victim of a psychological and not physical disorder, for they could only express their misgivings of scale and depth through language. As language was the ultimate path to truth and reason, to err from description and into illusion constituted madness.

The explanation of the sufferer that what they feel is different than the reality everyone else experiences clearly influences the diagnosis of vertigo as madness. This is less a dialogue between two people, so much as an external evaluation of the apparent evidence filtered through the received wisdom of the day. By this statement I simply want to highlight the contextual nature of 'scientific truths' and emphasise the position of the artist Terre Thaemlitz insofar as there is no truth beyond the function of particular meanings within specific contexts[9]. It would be overly simplistic to situate all discourse with the mentally ill at the beginning and end of the classical era. Yet the aim of the dialogue that did exist performs a cyclical return insofar as 'patients' were actually being listened to prior to and following the 'age of confinement'.

Compared to the incessant dialogue of reason and madness during the Renaissance, classical internment had been silencing. But it was not total: language was engaged in things rather than really suppressed. Confinement, prisons, dungeons, even tortures, engaged in a mute dialogue between reason and unreason - the dialogue of struggle. This dialogue itself was now disengaged; silence was absolute; there was no longer any common language between madness and reason; the language of delirium can be answered only by the absence of language, for delirium is not a fragment of dialogue with reason, it is not language at all...

Ibid. Foucault, p 261-62

9   Specific contexts;
Terre Thaemlitz, MONOCULTURE #39, Spring 2015

Opposite page: *Memorial to the Witches Burned at Finnmark, Norway.* **The memorial consists of two structures; an artwork by the late Louise Bourgeois and a building that houses records of the dead and their confessions by architect Peter Zumthor. Visited by the author during research for** *Here Comes Trouble.*

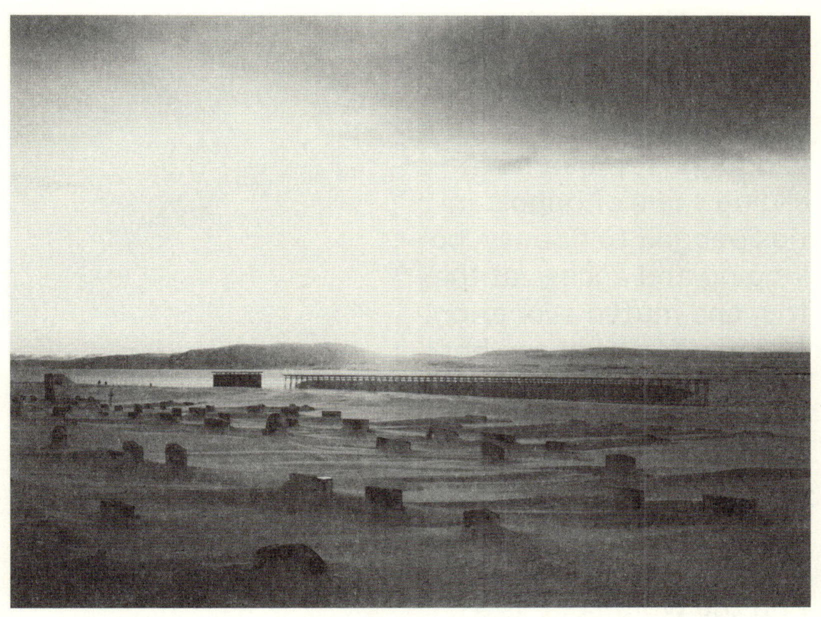

Marietta, Oluf Moring's wife
Brought before the court in Makkaur on   August 1 34

ACCUSED
of having cast a spell on Anders Mand by tying knots with pebbles in them on a piece of cloth
of having thrown stones into the sea when he sailed off, crying, 'Off you go, never to return '
of having made Oluf Paulsen lose an eye
of having done so because he was cross when she let her goats graze on his turf roof
of having cast a spell on late Laurits the Tailor due to an argument about a red skirt

DENIED KNOWING WITCHCRAFT
Said if she were to suffer, others would suffer too
Was subjected to the water ordeal and floated like a bob
Refused, still, to confess
Was found guilty on basis of denunciation and the water ordeal

Sentenced to death in fire at the stake
Was subsequently tortured

CONFESSED THEN
that she learnt witchcraft from Marrite Thamisdatter
that her apostle was called Old Lucifer
that she cast a spell on Laurits the Taylor by giving him a drink
that he immediately swelled up around the waist
that he died shortly afterwards

Excerpt from records provided at Steilneset - Note the confession only after torture.

As displaced persons the world over know all too well, language is both a gateway and a closed door. Language represents a sliding scale of opportunities pegged to fluency, belonging and access at the top, and muted alienation, and restriction at the bottom. The fascination with mangled dis-coherences, while politically and metaphysically interesting, has rarely become the purview of groups for whom 'getting the words out' is as much about legal representation as sense making, meaning and cultural orientation. Nonetheless the challenge and intrigue of cultural and political miscommunication remains. For me, this is a valid pursuit providing I avoid the dream of the artwork as some sort of conciliatory tower of babel.

Language is the first and last structure of madness, its constituent form; on language are based all the cycles in which madness articulates its nature. That the essence of madness can be ultimately defined in the simple structures of a discourse does not reduce it to a purely psychological nature, but gives it a hold over the totality of soul and body; such discourse is both silent language by which the mind speaks to itself in the truth proper to it, and the visible articulation of the movements of the body.

Michel Foucault, Madness and Civilisation: The History of Insanity in the Age of Reason, 1961 p 100

A site at which both forms of classical delirium (linguistic and physical) converge is the stutter. If the stutter is the point at which language jumps or bleeds out of the path of 'objective reason', I would assert that this linguistic deviation contains the key principles of a sorting mechanism, one which enacted systems of marking, naming and punishing within the era of socio-economic transition outlined in this chapter. The simplest and most general definition we can give of classical madness is indeed delirium: 'This word is derived from lira, a furrow; so that deliro actually means to move out of the furrow, away from the proper path of reason'.

Ibid. Foucault, p 99

To speak to or, worse, question the theologically endorsed economic logic of the period, or to utter words that could be interpreted as magical spells: each of such speech acts[10] served in the late renaissance and early classical periods as a means of routing out dissent and defamation against the desired, economically productive form. With the charges of 'heresy', 'witchcraft', 'vagrant' or 'madman' ringing through the collective conscious of Europe, it begs reason that any music, art, or new discovery was possible by the eighteenth-century at all. Indeed Galileo Galilei was forced to recount, such was the climate of fear. Yet many creative, investigative, radical minds were likely extinguished or else locked up

10   speech act;

'…in the terms of the philosopher J. L. Austin [ideology uses], 'performative rather than 'constative' language: it belongs to a class of speech acts which get something done (cursing, persuading, celebrating and so on) rather than to the discourse of a description. A pronouncement like 'Black is beautiful', popular in the days of the American civil rights movement, looks on the surface as though it is characterising a state of affairs, but it is in fact of course a rhetorical act of defiance and self-affirmation.'
Terry Eagleton, *Ideology, An Introduction*, 1991 p 19

41 And while they yet believed not for joy, and wondered, he said unto them, Have ye here any meat?

42 And they gave him a piece of a broiled fish, and of an honeycomb.

43 And *w*he took *it*, and did eat before them.

44 And he said unto them, *x*These *are* the words which I spake unto you, while I was yet with you, that all things must be fulfilled which were written in the law of Moses, and *in* the prophets, and *in* the psalms, concerning me.

45 Then *y*opened he their understanding, that they might understand the Scriptures,

46 And said unto them, Thus it is written, and thus it behoved Christ to suffer, and to rise from the dead the third day:

47 And that repentance and *z*remis-sion of sins should be preached in his name among *a*all nations, beginning at Jerusalem.

48 And *b*ye are witnesses of these things.

49 ¶ And, *c*behold, I send the promise of my Father upon you: but tarry ye in the city of Jerusalem, until ye be endued with power from on high.

50 ¶ And he led them out as far as to Bethany; and he lifted up his hands, and blessed them.

51 And *d*it came to pass, while he blessed them, he was parted from them, and carried up into heaven.

52 And they worshipped him, and returned to Jerusalem with great joy:

53 And were continually *e*in the temple, praising and blessing God. Amen.

A.D. 33.

CHAP. 24.
w Acts 10. 41.
x Matt. 16. 21.
y Mark 9. 31.
   Acts 16. 14.
   2 Cor. 4. 6.
z Dan. 9. 24.
a Gen. 12. 3.
   Ps. 22. 27.
   Isa. 49. 6.
   Jer. 31. 34.
   Hos. 2. 23.
   Micah 4. 2.
   Mal. 1. 11.
   Gal. 3. 14.
b John 15. 27.
   Acts 1. 22.
c Isa. 44. 3.
   Joel 2. 28.
   Acts 2. 1.
d Eph. 1. 20.
e Acts 2. 46.

THE GOSPEL ACCORDING TO

St. JOHN.

CHAPTER 1.

The divinity and incarnation of Christ.

IN the beginning was *a*the Word, and the Word was *b*with God, and *c*the Word was God.

2 The same was in the beginning with God.

3 All things were made by him; and without him was not any thing made that was made.

4 In him was life; and the life was the light of men.

5 And *d*the light shineth in darkness; and the darkness comprehended it not.

6 ¶ There *e*was a man sent from God, whose name *was* John.

7 The same came for a witness, to bear witness of the Light, that all *men* through him might believe.

8 He *f*was not that Light, but *was sent* to bear witness of that Light.

9 *That g*was the true Light, which lighteth every man that cometh into the world.

10 He was in the world, and *h*the world was made by him, and the world knew him not.

11 He *i*came unto his own, and his own received him not.

12 But *j*as many as received him, to them gave he 1power to become the sons of God, *even* to them that believe on his name:

13 Which were born, not of blood, nor of the will of the flesh, nor of the will of man, *k*but of God.

A.D. 26.

CHAP. 1.
a Rev. 19. 13.
b Zech. 13. 7.
c Isa. 9. 6.
   Phil. 2. 6.
d ch. 3. 19.
e Mal. 3. 1.
f Acts 13. 25.
g Isa. 49. 6.
h Ps. 33. 6.
   1 Cor. 8. 6.
i Luke 19. 14.
j Isa. 56. 5.
   Rom. 8. 15.
   2 Pet. 1. 4.
1 Or, the right, or, privilege.
k Deut. 30. 6.
   Jas. 1. 18.
l Matt. 1. 20.
   1 Tim. 3. 16.
m Rom. 1. 3.
n Heb. 2. 14.
o Isa. 40. 5.
   Matt. 17. 2.
p Col. 2. 3.
q Col. 1. 17.
r Eph. 1. 6.
s Ex. 20. 1.
t Rom. 5. 21.
u ch. 14. 6.
v Ex. 33. 20.
w 1 John 4. 9.
x Pro. 8. 30.
y Mal. 4. 5.
z Luke 1. 17.
2 Or, a prophet.
a Isa. 40. 3.

14 And *l*the Word *m*was made *n*flesh, and dwelt among us, (and we *o*beheld his glory, the glory as of the only begotten of the Father,) full *p*of grace and truth.

15 ¶ John bare witness of him, and cried, saying, This was he of whom I spake, He that cometh after me is preferred before me: for *q*he was before me.

16 And of his *r*fulness have all we received, and grace for grace.

17 For the *s*Law was given by Moses, *t*but grace and *u*truth came by Jesus Christ.

18 No *v*man hath seen God at any time; the *w*only begotten Son, which is in *x*the bosom of the Father, he hath declared *him*.

19 ¶ And this is the record of John, when the Jews sent priests and Levites from Jerusalem to ask him, Who art thou?

20 And he confessed, and denied not; but confessed, I am not the Christ.

21 And they asked him, What then? Art thou *y*Elias? And he saith, *z*I am not. Art thou 2that prophet? And he answered, No.

22 Then said they unto him, Who art thou? that we may give an answer to them that sent us. What sayest thou of thyself?

23 He said, I *am* the voice of one crying in the wilderness, Make straight the way of the Lord, as said *a*the prophet Esaias.

89

THE King James translation of the Gospel according to John begins with the well-known passage, "In the beginning was the Word, and the Word was with God, and the Word was God." The 'Word' referred to is translated from the Koine Greek 'Logos.' The meaning and the consequence of this translation is one that is still being discussed today. Through different translations or different readings, this short sentence, which has become a central idea to the Christian faith and has influenced the lives of millions of believers, could take on multiple meanings. The ambiguity of the sentence is at the heart of the problem. You could translate the same passage as, "...the Word was a God." It could also be read as, "...the Word was Divine." You could even take the reading "...God was the Word," with each variation containing subtle but quite important differences to their meaning.

The "Word" is seen by many as a description of Jesus Christ, and this particular passage holds an important aspect of the understanding of belief in the Holy Trinity. John goes on to say, "the Word was made flesh and dwelt among us ...full of grace and truth." Christ is seen as the medium through which the word of God is translated to us; the humanising link to divine ideas and principles.

The translation of the word Logos that causes the biggest problem is the fact that beyond "word" and "language," it can also be read as, "thought" or "idea." It is impossible to imagine language without thought or vice-versa; the two are inherently connected but they have their own very separate meanings. A thought is internal and outside of language but language is needed to translate or externalise all thought. This seems to fit with the concept of belief in the Holy Trinity, with God the Father, Christ the son and the Holy Spirit, existing as a single entity; both the idea and its translation into language capable of human understanding. However when dual meaning within one word exists, it opens the possibility for fundamental misreading and for serious misunderstanding. John 1:1 could, therefore be read as "...and God was the Idea." A different interpretation that could fundamentally alter our beliefs.

We must also consider the ideas Jacques Derrida introduces in *Of Grammatology* regarding the translation of Logos. The bringing of ideas into physical existence, the "signification of the sign"; speech, alphabetic text, physical movement or the creation of images; the translation of ideas through a form of 'writing'. Derrida speaks of our inability to translate; a point when the signifier can reach the complete sign is impossible. However he also suggests that perhaps this is not only the failure of language, but also the inability of the human mind to comprehend something written. Language is limited by comparison to the immense possibility contained within an idea therefore misreading is inevitable.

It is not possible to express the truth of an idea in a physical state; the nature of thought means that writing will never be enough. However, at the same moment, the nature of writing means that the mind will never be able to fully comprehend either. We can never get to a truth itself, a fine example being the confusion surrounding the multiple meanings contained within a word such as 'Logos'. Both words and ideas are incapable of a definitive understanding of one another. We must be careful to understand that even within our own thoughts there is an inability to reach a central whole.

A true meaning cannot even be fully present in the signified. For one fully complete idea or a true present whole meaning to exist all others would be excluded. Humanity is unable to aspire to understand such perfection in thought; our minds are designed for misinterpretation and the creation of a new individual understanding of a new and individual sign. These ideas when looked at in parallel to belief in Christian faith open some interesting questions.

We, as humans, can never reach the whole and full meaning contained within the divine Logos. The only possibility of this would be through God. But if we consider what we have discussed, God can only possibly exist through the translation of human ideas into 'writing', therefore the possibility of an individual, true, divine idea of God; one totally intelligible, is unachievable. God exists in a translation of translated ideas within the human mind, which is itself not fully capable of a complete comprehension. We take on belief in God through our own fundamental mistranslation, the idea of a central and complete Logos is as flawed as the image we have of God contained within the page of a holy text. Such a page is created in his "image and likeness." It is as accurate a description as we humans will ever reach, but more than that, it is the only possibility that God, the divine logos, has for a physical existence. If God can only exist in 'writing', or the translation of ideas; what you hold in your hand is in fact his reality. Of all the religious iconography created as an attempt to depict to us the image of our creator, it could be seen that the most accurate is in fact the book itself; an imperfect translation of an imperfect but eternal idea, one central to our very existence as human beings. "In the beginning was the Word," and it will continue to be there until the end, regardless of the questions surrounding its 'truth'.

until the condition for which they were being 'treated' became their inevitable fate [11]. For instance: 'it is a standard psychiatric concept, [that] if you put people in isolation, they will go insane', said psychiatrist Sandra Schank who was quoted in *How to Survive Solitary Confinement*, Nautilus Scientific Journal, 2016.

Language is my greatest tool and can be my most awful weapon. Awesome in its capacity to deceive even the speaker of their own thoughts a la Freudian slip; I am trapped by language only until the point at which I make it detract from its sense-making role… in chanting, moaning, screaming, swallowing and shouting:

> *The stutter engenders a withdrawal, literally, which is to say that the words are triggered but trapped, the mouth cavity holds and harbours them. As a consequence a stutter is a threat to coherence, to the established course, to smooth flow; it proliferates the mouth that utters even while idle. In this context, the stutter is the eruption which reminds us of the already existing stutter. The somatic stutter reveals the metaphoric one. As Barthes states regarding the music of a text, 'It is both what is expressed and implicit in the text: what is pronounced but not articulated'.*

Christoph Migone, *Sonic Somatic*, 2011 p 136-7

Language, or perhaps just noise, is only one way of reading or rather, 'listening' to deviant knowledge production. Sociologically speaking, a foreign utterance will always be read as either art and/or insanity depending on one's listener. The thin line between insanity and creative genius represents the final reckoning for the treatment of delirious discourse by shackles, confinement and paternalistic study for Foucault. Who, Foucault asks, would have confined the celebrated minds of Nietzsche, Van Gogh or Artaud? A list to which we might also add Plath, Walker and Woolf. Foucault concludes that while mental illness has become

Opposite page;
Robert Heatherington, *The Word Made Flesh*, 2012, two-page insert courtesy of the artist.

11   Inevitable fate;
Those accused of witchcraft were often tested by the water-method. This entailed the victim being tied up and thrown in a body of water: if they sank, they were innocent (thus, they died); if they floated, they were witches (and were put to death by fire).

an increasing malady for writers and artists, it is the work of art that separates the artist from the edge of dissolution into madness, the contour against the void, '...a fundamental absence of language, ... the sheer cliff over the abyss of the work's absence.'

Michel Foucault, *Madness and Civilisation: The History of Insanity in the Age of Reason*, 1961 p 287

Finally, to conclude this particular nonlinear example, the voice of the patient represents a welcome return for Foucault:

> *This is why we must do justice to Freud. ...Freud went back to madness at the level of its language, reconstituted one of the essential elements of an experience reduced to silence by positivism; he did not make a major addition to the list of psychological treatments for madness; he restored, in medical thought, the possibility of a dialogue with unreason.*

Ibid. Foucault, p 188

A Double Articulation

In a very real way, two significant nonlinear historical trajectories can be drawn from Foucault's study into the treatment of mental illness[12]: 1. the cyclical economic collapse of the workhouse model of containment, and 2. the suppression and return of dialogue with the mentally disabled at the end of the renaissance and then, again, in modern psychiatry.

There are different types of nonlinearity; those tied up with negative feedback, which in turn may be read within economic, social or other processes; and those that critique the idea of 'human progress'. It is this latter critique that I refer to in the examples immediately above.

I would like to highlight the expression of economic desirability, ascribed directly upon the heads of the populous, outlined as

12   Illness;
Silvia Federici's work into medieval European and contemporary witch hunting in parts of Africa can also be read as tragic, nonlinear cycles of history.

13   Minor tonalities;
Stewart Hall talking to Laurie Taylor about the Post Colonial theorist Edward Said, during a special programme dedicated to late Stewart Hall on *Thinking Allowed*, BBC Radio 4, 2011.

an organisational process of negative feedback in correlation with the diagrams illustrated above. This is a process in which, those unable or unwilling to participate economically, have been habitually sorted-out of society proper. In order to do this, a site, opportunity and platform for protest had to be denied those who had the most to lose from such a process.

As Edward Said liked to say, 'history operates in the manner of a baroque melody… it is composed of both the major and the minor tonalities'[13]. Thus, as the second part of a double articulation that amplifies both a longer trend in social organisation, and the subjective experiences of the mentally disabled, deviant knowledge can be found at the heart of mental illnesses' identification and justification. This includes the identification of delirious speech explored above.

In the previous chapter, I sought to locate the deviancy or radicality within a socially oriented art project, which concluded that truly deviant knowledge might, in fact, be that which exceeds the capacity for an object to be recognised at all. This may be directly related to an argument around the question of whether God is the word, or that, on the contrary, that which transcends language cannot itself be named. If this were at one time the case for the hegemonic powers of the West, the divine logos of the mental sufferer, once perhaps (mis)taken for speaking in tongues, has, during the Enlightenment, become shackled to the iron logic of 'science'. Here, in a direct parallel with the role of dialogue within such socially oriented artistic endeavours, an analysis of speech-deviation, the murmur, stutter but also the

14   Itself;

'Measured by their functional value alone, the creation of the houses of confinement can be regarded as a failure. Their disappearance throughout Europe, at the beginning of the nineteenth-century, as receiving centres for the indigent and prisons of poverty, was to sanction their ultimate failure: a transitory and ineffectual remedy, a social precaution clumsily formulated by a nascent industrialisation. And yet, in this very failure, the classical period conducted an irreducible experiment. What appears to us today as a clumsy dialectic of production and prices then possessed its real meaning as a certain ethical consciousness of labour, in which the difficulties of the economic mechanism lost their urgency in favour of the affirmation of value.'

Ibid, Foucault, p 55. I have extended this quote as it resonates in a very slight but telling way with my experience of the ZEITBANK project, discussed above, i.e. when socio-cultural or material gratification is achieved through a relatively direct formula or investment and return, it is easy to misplace a sense of proportion. Time and again, unregulated investors go bust.

content of dialogue are understood as crucial components in the history of mental disability. Deviant speech, as such, is recurrent in a precisely nonlinear cycle of exploratory practices.

These practices eventually became known as modern psychiatry, or rather, the birth of modern psychiatry heralds a full rotation of the practice of 'patient' consultation.

The stable states I can identify at the beginning and end of Michel Foucault's investigation into the treatment of the mentally disabled, involve an adherence to the particularities of the mentally disabled, though in very different guises, through spoken dialogue. If we return now to his text, a series of examples may be drawn in order to demonstrate my observations. Multiple models of the role of deviancy can be garnered from Foucault's *Madness and Civilisation*, as deviant exploration abides by a process of renewal, exploration and discovery. If the entire arc of the development of psychiatry, from the Renaissance perception of the mentally ill as inspired, spirited and animalistic, through the classical period of exclusion and experimentation, to the modern treatment of insanity as a form of disease, were to be conceived of as 'human progress', then the violent interstice of division and exclusion (or bifurcation and transition to phase change) could, disturbingly, be conceptualised as an inherently creative period of social medicalisation. However, we should understand this reading as somewhat perverse itself; the violent 'treatment' (which was more or less punishment from the contemporary perspective) of the mentally ill has been clouded by different rationalisations throughout its history. The 'houses of correction' were established, not as medical institutions but as socially normative apparatus coupled to a moral statement concerning the virtue of labour itself [14].

As an example of nonlinear dynamics at play within the story of mental illness, we need only observe the decline of the great houses of confinement under economic pressures. This is to say that their true virtue for society becomes clear when, in parallel to

15 Ibid. Foucault, p 51

lax competition provided by the workhouse, poverty was created in one area on the pretext of suppressing it in another, reproducing, whether intentionally or not, the exact conditions of the re-absorption of surplus labour at a lower cost in wages.

Again, this might be an all too tidy picture of how the political economics driving changes in labour relations, production and deviancy intermesh within the seventeenth-century. However, as an attempt to abstract and conceptualize the problem of large-scale European manufacturing as it experienced cycles of boom and bust[16], let's try reviewing the case through the lens of the thermodynamic models previously discussed. The process through which energy enters into the system correlates to a surplus of labour; human energy is organised to work like temperature effectors in a refrigerator in an attempt to produce a stable civic environment. This happens by locking deviant (non-productive) individuals into production chains within the workhouse. Their surplus labour is used to regulate flows of energy into and out of the system in the form of profit margins that incentivise such institutional organisation. The streets are swept of vagrants, but their energy is still flowing into the system.

Yet, with the unchecked use of prison labour, the economic pressures of oversupply and lack-of-demand counter-reacted creating instabilities, market slumps and the consequential decline of the overall environment within which these nonlinear processes unfolded. Having achieved little in the way of social stability, the organisational system of the workhouse collapsed by the end of the eighteenth-century. Despite workhouse failure in the past in Europe, today, in America, new markets have opened up in the form of the prison-industrial-complex, wherein the 'nation' of the prison only gets stronger the more inmates it takes in. Though the behaviour this particularity demonstrates is cyclical, in a Marxist reading of 'primitive accumulation'[17], it merely represents another round of ever tighter controls meted out by the state or hegemony upon its citizenry, most likely on behalf of profiteering influences.

---

16   Boom and Bust;
'The first houses of correction were opened in England during a full economic recession [in 1610]. …But what had been a moral requirement became an economic tactic when commerce and industry recovered after 1651.' Ibid. Foucault, p 52

17   Primitive Accumulation;
Primitive accumulation is the process by which one piles up fortunes in money rather than land on the one hand, and the creation of a propertyless proletariat on the other. It is the separation of the producers from the means by which they can maintain themselves.

As an illustration of how the social model of deviance operates throughout the parameters of his text, Foucault's study of the treatment of mental illness demonstrates a repeated process through which dominant groups attempt to reproduce the conditions, socio-economic or otherwise, which serve to maintain their own advantage. Another, more explicitly violent form of regulation, exists in the layered and often contradictory metaphysics that supported and legitimised the persecution and execution of witches during this period, and described the persecuted thus:

> *You are the true Hyenas, that allure us with the fairness of your skins and when folly has brought us within your reach, you leap upon us. You are the traitors of Wisdom, the **impediment to industry**... the clogs to virtue and the goads that drive us to all vices, impiety and ruin. You are the Fool's Paradise, the wiseman's Plague and the Grand Error of Nature*

Walter Charleton, Ephesian Matron, 1659, quoted in Federici, p 163 author's emphasis

Thus rang the hollow persecutory charge of one type of religious damnation. These charges echo the ideas that would strip and route the working peasant woman into the home and send the newly formed male European proletariat to his newly ascribed role.

In DeLanda's model of the particularities of social strata formation, those who have gained privileged access to certain roles find ways to reproduce those conditions over generations. The naming of a subject as 'deviant' is a natural consequence of the sorting criteria by which these dominant groups organise members of society into formalised categories. Interestingly, DeLanda also observes that in order for hierarchical social systems to crystallise (in the manner typical of the above period), a secondary consolidation of individuals into formalised groups needs to occur. Here, the ascription of social roles and positionalities takes on a theological or legal definition that solidifies the sorting criteria into abstract social class systems. In that vein, Foucault's study is structured by literary and other examples of 'high culture' and Federici tackles the complex manifestation of the period of European proletarianisation between the Late Medieval and Early Classical periods as an 'ideological bricolage'. These two forms of designation (ideology critique and high culture) solidify class structure by delimiting access to knowledge in complex terminology.

Taken as an arc of urban architectural and institutional development, the treatment of mental illness, though by no means exclusively, can be understood as an expression of the enhanced ambitions and material capacity of Europe during the late renaissance and early modernism. Developments within the built environment, insofar as they are coupled to the institutional organisations that govern them, are products of regulated flows of material and labour energy.

Furthermore, economic analysis can be used to explain the ascription and treatment of social deviancy. From an analogy wherein organisational capacity is enhanced through intercalary elements and replicators formed by autocatalytic loops, the social expression of gathering, coupling and, finally, consolidating different forms of behaviour, skills and attitudes coheres with a bourgeois sensibility toward mental disability and labour.

Additionally, the bourgeois sensibility toward the wealth of a nation as the volume of its citizens, expressed by Henry IV's statement that the strength and wealth of a king lie in the number and opulence of his citizens[18], is directly correlated to a set of organisa-

18   Citizens;
Silvia Federici, *Caliban and the Witch: Woman the Body and Primitive Accumulation*, 2004 p 87

tional principles that sought to promote the full employment of its male citizens and the oppression of women into machines of reproduction. Thus, the men and women who did not fulfil their productive roles were labelled deviant.

<u>Chapter Conclusion - Dialogue with Unreason</u>

Is the unnameable within language or outside it? If that which is truly deviant knowledge is situated out-of-bounds, in what manner should I prepare myself for its emergence? Can there be a utility to deviant knowledge? In the history of witch hunting, the sober fact that by demonising undesirable groups of women, by reducing all forms of traditional magic and medicine to a pact with the devil, an expedient was created to that typologies' destruction. For Silvia Federici, the paradoxical knot that bound victims to the stake was that this very devil, acted as a double agent of God himself. In a sense, then, the devil brought a certain binary structure to the world, organising any form of transgression into either devilish or godly forces.

With deviancy, context is everything. As a label, the term is a very different thing among cultural and theoretical circles than it is in the juridical hands of state powers. The form of belief or behaviour that would lead the state to add one to a watch list (which is to say, the type of deviancy I am interested in) is dangerously ambiguous, permitting the devil to be unearthed wherever one points one's accusatorial finger, in support of the norms of the times. Paradoxically, although I too desire to blur, distort and make deviancy more ambiguous, I wish to do so at the service of the accused. By way of drawing attention to the degree of ambiguity necessary for the undifferentiated persecution of 'evil', a fleshing out of the term aims at enhancing the political imagination and, in turn, creating jurors capable of suspending judgement until this dimension has been considered.

Undifferentiated state violence very often involves the dehumanising of the violated party. When internal, spatial and psychological repression becomes the order of the day, equally dehumanising forces become masked in scientific, theological and other academic debates. The raw reality is right there before us: in the transition from one stage of capitalism to another, nothing is sacred but the upward flow of surplus labour.

If deviancy has a utility, then, is it only as a means of sorting, consolidating and discarding difference? This is a question of political stance; either you see human nature as greedy and self serving or inherently pleased by the pleasure of others and therefore prone to acting benevolently whenever possible. As anthropologist David Graeber writes, the problem is, it only takes a few self-serving greedy agents to bring ones' otherwise benevolent stance into practical redundancy.

If the ascription of racial, social or ideological transgression acts as a 'primitive step-back' before a 'great leap forward' for capital, it is of crucial import to maintain a lively debate around the distinction, definition and ascription of philosophical, theological, cultural or political deviancy.

Alas, room for debate, or open and free dialogue is arguably no longer possible under the basic principle that it occurs in privacy between two or more persons. What I type, email, text or say to another person via contemporary information technology, no longer happens privately between the recipient and myself. Arguably, this technology cannot ensure my freedom of expression where '…that liberty has not only to be understood as individual independence but as being part of a larger group of free individuals. It's not only to the will of a single subject but to the existence of a common space, a stage where everyone is at the same time the actor and audience and ensures his own freedom by giving reciprocal recognition to the others freedom. [This is what Hannah] Arendt calls public space[19].'

19   Space;
Jonas Marx, The Prism, *The Anxious Prop Case 5: The Intellectual Property Issue*, 2013 p 20, 22

1

So wrote Jonas Marx in the aftermath of the Snowden revelations in 2013. Marx went on to conclude that,

> *When a technical system demands to cover the complete human sphere - like Big Data does - public space vanishes. And this is what makes the prism so dangerous. You might not feel any restraints personally because it does not affect you personally - at first sight. But, by eliminating the openness of spaces for subject-subject interactions, which are not are not mediated by any technical determinations, it eliminates our political freedom.*

Ibid. Marx p 22

As the demonisation of groups who sin against the historically constructed, narrow idea of what passes for Western European Culture threatens to increase, it would be wise to explore the larger picture and to ask, who benefits from this apparent conflict of cultures?

I have tried to locate my arguments in broad, physical, historical arguments in order to contribute to a sober debate around difference, deviancy and persecution. If, in the fifteenth, sixteenth and seventeenth-centuries, hegemonic forces permitted and institutionalised the confinement, torture and public execution of those who held subversive thoughts, what contemporary social engineering processes would be necessary to clear the way for the next 'great leap of capital'? Clearly, there are no straightforward answers to the complex intermesh of pressures and personal quarrels that seek resolution within religious and political purges. Through mindfulness, the pursuit of wordless knowledge, comes presence. In my relatively optimistic view, it will be the cultural nuances (and not turgid national and religious differences) that cause our undoing as a differentiated mass. On the stage of the demographically textured global city, we must learn and continue to act with the collective agency of the group, and not allow the next geo-economic or environmental upheaval to simply become another opportunity

for states, corporations and individuals to settle accounts. Therefore it is the artwork (in the broadest sense) that must seek out that
peripheral cultural arena that exists in Michel Foucault's imaginary,
moments before the void. In this sense, I'm with Martin Heidegger
in so far as, in *Being and Time* (1927), he suggests that even though
a doctrine may happen to be true, I should return to the source from
which it originally sprung. Heidegger also believed that this rethinking inevitably modifies the inherited doctrine to some extent.
How else can I think, but in relation to the concerns of the day?

We have to question our a-priori assertions, down to the deep-
est level. To negate this challenge would permit others to take that
liberty from us. He therefore asks us, what is knowledge? What is it
to know something or someone? What is a knower?

Despite the physical constraints of the material world, it is
as courageous, conscious beings that we have been formed. On a
subjective level, to ignore pain is to ignore ones' own humanity.
However, taking pleasure in another person's pain has been right-
fully diagnosed as a form of mental disability belonging to the field
of psychopathology. In my view, mental illness can be defined as an
inability to conceptualise another person's suffering.

Spatializing and Politicizing Deviancy

In this work, I have tried to analyse the way in which deviancy has been historically ascribed and how the treatment of those bearing its title has been legitimised. Parallel to this, I have offered the reader a series of reflections upon a pressing, European, socio-political arena, within which the traits, fears and repressive violence which historically contextualise the ascription of deviancy, have begun to increase.

To complete this theoretical work I will now attempt to apply the methodology I have developed, a kind of philosophical systems analysis, to a set of short problems. My conclusion will therefore attempt to make a precise reflection on the core themes that I find at the heart of my work and thought; in this final chapter I aim once again, to spatialise, philosophically question and politicize the term deviancy.

The methodology I have used sought to identify two or more 'stable states' and an area of transition between these two spatio-temporal, or political fixities. Between the feudal and capitalist systems of organisation I have argued, as others have before me, a process of violent political consolidation occurred across Europe. The evidence for this is written into the very language we use, such as in the word faggot, referenced above, as well as in state/public, citizen, and cultural records.

Furthermore, the repression and servitude installed within the human psyche during this period, haunts many of us in the continuing bourgeois economic, colonial relation of master and slave, abstracted for the West in the form of the debt fuelled working day.

Where credit or money performs as the 'intercalary element' (in place of dialogue, questioning and material communication), these pitiless labour relations, that would drive you and me to the slave-master relation given the slightest opportunity, can only worsen. Yet, there is always the potential to do things differently, providing a meaningful space exists into which new, deviant forms may proliferate.

Spatializing Deviancy

Searching for music is like searching for God. They're very similar, there's an effort to reclaim the unmentionable, the unsayable, the seeable, the unspeakable, all those things, comes into being a composer and writing music. Searching for notes, and pieces of musical information that don't exist.

David Bowie, *Verbatim*, Archive on 4, BBC Radio 4, 2016

My opening claim for this paper constituted a scale shift between the behaviour of social entities and thermodynamic activity, involving entropy (measured as the disorder or 'chaos' of a body of molecules). This measurement of chaos is equivalent, in the scientific study of the universe, with a lack of information when determining the rate of entropy within a given thermodynamic system. Having made my leap of faith into the world of physics, I have correlated this (so far) non-qualifiable (or absence of) data within classical thermodynamics with the naming, fear-of and subsequent attempt to control the unknown.

I have speculated that in order to re-organise a social body the 'unknown' has been both 'edited out' of socio-economic society proper (as shown by Michel Foucault) and used to instil fear and a culture of violence within a revolutionary populous (as outlined by Silvia Federici).

In physics, one form of 'known unknowns' is 'dark matter'. Science knows it is there from the way it affects other elements. However, as the information used to decipher dark matter is measured in terms of light, its absence is documented as a shadow upon human endeavour[1]. Dark matter sounds, to me, rather ominous, but there are other, less demonic sounding, physical events that occur at

1   Endeavour;
Lisa Randall - author of *Dark Matter and the Dinosaurs: The Astounding Interconnectedness of the Universe*, talking on *Free Thinking*, BBC Radio 3, January, 2015

the very edge of human scientific knowledge. In fact, what has been historically spatialised as deviancy, i.e locked up and persecuted, I would argue, is actually difference exiled in the name of deviance.

What I am arguing for, in the end, is to stop the exile and to open up a space for deviancy: a space for the unknown, a space for the lack of information and the possibility of chaos, a space for dark matter to be understood despite its seeming antagonism to our current human capabilities. Like Bowie, I am also sympathetic to the idea that the really deviant doesn't exist (yet), but that we search after it nonetheless… and that we might find hints of it in the space of our creations.

In his recent Reith Lecture for the BBC, the acclaimed theoretical physicist and cosmologist, Stephen Hawkins used a dirty joke to draw his audience's attention to a form of cosmological enquiry that would, given his severe physical and vocal impediments, likely have had him burnt at the stake for heresy a few centuries earlier. Hawkins' lecture focused on a magnificent problem that occupies a key parameter to the human understanding of the physical universe. His introduction went as follows: 'When John Wheeler introduced the term "black hole" in 1967 it replaced the earlier name, "frozen star." Wheelers' coinage emphasised that the remnants of collapsed stars are of interest independently of how they are formed. The new name caught on quickly, it suggested something dark and mysterious but the French, being French, saw a more risqué meaning.' (Stephen Hawkins, *Do Black Holes Have No Hair?*, BBC Reith Lecture, part one of two, February, 2016)

To paraphrase Hawkins; from the outside, one cannot tell what created a black hole. From the outside, a black hole only exhibits information about its total mass, the state of rotation, and electronic charge. 'John Wheeler is famous for expressing this principle as "A Black Hole has no hair" …To the French, this just confirmed their suspicions.' (Ibid. Hawkins)

The reason I picked up on this, aside from the clue it gives toward the limitless scope of human ambition (Hawkins believes the only chance for human survival is to move to another planet), is that if we can spatialise deviancy, then perhaps we can get closer to understanding how it functions for the human mind and body political. This adds to a serious argument against the ascription of deviancy as a process of naming that inevitably leads to undifferentiated repression and violence. If the 'most intelligent person on earth' would have been burnt at the stake under the auspices of a previous regime of 'reason', how can it ever be justified to foster demonising, literal and metaphorical witch hunts against nonconformists, on the premise that one simply doesn't understand the types of knowledge they live by?

In short, I think the virtue of an analogy between human thought, social anxieties and black holes lies, yet again, in classical thermodynamics. Gigantic stars can collapse in on themselves under their own gravity; indeed this is what creates black holes in the first place. However, as an object of study, I would like to revert to this phenomenon's previous name and call it a frozen star, for the moment. This highlights these entities as cognitively fixed, yet generating unknown, arrested and thus deviant knowledge.

A frozen star has a boundary called the event horizon. Here, gravity is strong enough to grab light back, preventing it from escaping. To an external observer someone going into a frozen star would appear to slow down and then hover upon the event horizon where their image would fade, becoming redder and redder until disappearing from sight entirely. (Ibid. Hawkins) According to Hawkins, when a frozen star is created by gravitational collapse, it rapidly settles down to a stationary state, which is characterised by only three parameters: the mass, angular momentum and electronic charge. Apart from these properties, a frozen star preserves no other details of the object that collapsed. And this, excitingly, is correlated, by scientists to a measure in entropy, as the loss or lack of information of a frozen star's origin.

A mathematical discovery in 1970 revealed that the surface area of the event horizon has a property that always increases when additional matter or radiation falls into the frozen star. These properties suggest that there is a correlation between the area of the event horizon of a frozen star and thermodynamics: specifically, the concept of entropy and thermodynamic entropy.

Entropy can be graded by a measurement of the disorder of a system or equivalently as a lack of knowledge of the precise state of a system's particles.

The famous second law states that entropy always increases with time. This discovery was the first hint of this crucial connection.

Ibid. Hawkins

The measure of the entropy of a frozen star would therefore be the measure of the amount of information lost when the frozen star was created. However, classical thermodynamics also states that energy cannot be created or destroyed, only transformed. This would imply that a frozen star could be in equilibrium with a thermal radiation some temperature other than zero. According to classical concepts no such equilibrium is possible since the frozen star would absorb any thermal radiation that fell into it, but, by definition, would not be able to emit anything in return. It cannot emit anything; it cannot emit heat. (Ibid. Hawkins)

This is the paradox of the frozen star, for, according to the second law of thermodynamics, all heat energy cools through inertia. This inertia can only be postponed by an external source of energy, such as the sun. As a frozen star would suck any thermal energy into it, and therefore away from the event horizon, the classical laws of thermodynamics begin to break down. This is paradoxical because the very formula developed to interpret frozen stars sets the conditions of its own undoing.

But the real paradox is that thermal equilibrium is, by definition, the end state of thermo-molecular motion, which produces a temperature of zero. Thermal motion increases upon the event horizon of the frozen star, at an apparent equilibrium, without becoming transformed into a new energetic state or reaching thermal zero. Therefore, the thermal residue or transformed energy must emerge somewhere, and scientists (maybe we should just call them thinkers) have speculated that this occurs in universes parallel to ours.

The event horizon of a frozen star therefore represents not only the limits of our understanding of this cosmic phenomenon, but also challenges the most basic principles about the predictability of the universe and the certainty of history. (Ibid. Hawkins) If god is a thing we cannot know, is god, then, a frozen star?

<u>Politicising Deviancy</u>
As an intellectual exercise I have entertained analogies between frozen stars (now officially known as 'black holes'), and a spiritual discourse around the nature of the universe itself. This has also led to reflection around Bowies' conception of God as the unknowable, an idea to be found throughout theological, mystical and ancient 'secret' histories. With the name change from 'frozen star' to 'black hole', we are forced to acknowledge the space of some big unknowns.

I might argue that 'trouble' takes the form of the pronounced limits of human thought about the universe. But then… perhaps trouble is only in the limits and deviancy lies just outside of them? In any case, rather than conclude my paper by explaining the ascription of deviancy away, by making deviancy disappear into a theoretical concept of itself, it is necessary to locate the sociological problem of deviancy as an on-going issue.

Sociologically, I can make deviancy seem to disappear into criminality, or simply difference, or otherness. However, it is important to get involved, to serve supposition with empirical evidence, and, finally, to pursue scientific method in a fashion befitting the nineteenth-century Russian anarchist-revolutionary, Michael Bakunin. In his colourful life that included, amongst a string of political uprisings and an escape from a Siberian labour camp,

> *'[Bakunin] considered scientific method very useful [though] he sharply opposed 'scientific despotism' as demoralising to an even greater degree than the despotism of violence, because it corrupted man's thought at its source. The most degrading slavery to which mankind could ever be subjected would be a society ruled by pedants.'*

Michael Bakunin *Selected Writings*, edited by Arthur Lehning, 1973 p 17

I should also countercheck my own left wing political biases. In my view, liberal academia has been rightly criticised for tending to explain-away social and criminal problems engendered by racial and cultural differences, or else simply to ignore them from an ivory tower. In any case it is never a bad idea to try to take a sober look at one's political biases. The trouble is, as demonstrated by an attempt to spatialise my concept of deviancy in my conclusion, a close inspection of deviant knowledge easily ushers me away to the liminal, quasi-science fictional, hyper theoretical realm.

Rather than neutralising differences that are a meaningful part of the composition of social (or class) and cultural (or racial) conflict, terminology that would constitute a meaningful engagement needs to expand upon the existing terrain. Perhaps conflict, in the form of discussion, across social and cultural barriers would serve to make explicit the more painful realities about the ascription of deviancy.

Perhaps these discussions would reveal more precisely that the ascription of deviancy is used to legitimate violence and, as such, constitutes a form of violence in itself. This won't heal social wounds, but it may help to create situations whereby a mutual rejection of base, naming processes are facilitated through any number of shared communicative activities.

To conclude, in writing this paper, I have explored the scientific premise that entropy attends to all matter. Our history will be what we make of it depending on how one responds to the condition of entropy. By locating the consequential changes of entropy within linear or non-linear conceptions of history, we in turn shape that history. Without deviation from the norm, there would be no new forms. Without contested parameters, any assertion of form is meaningless.

In the study of physics, chaos and disorder express deviant behaviour that is either regulated or else simply goes on increasing. In nature, chaos and disorder necessitate and facilitate adaptive behaviour. Human life is not the only story of the natural world. If Hawkins' prediction that humanity will only be able to support life on another planet one-hundred years from now, we had better work out how to get along until then! This could be the most important phase transition our species has ever known. In order to escape the teleological narrative arc of near-certain extinction in earth bound human life, non-linear narratives have been made available by information and systems analysis. Without these models, history is liable to be recounted from limited, binary chrono-logical perspectives of events. I think we can do more.

The right parameters are fundamental to observations on which non-linear analytic models can be elaborated. They signal a means of identifying morphology and stages of transition between what may otherwise seem like black and white examples. If we are to comprehend our situation in anything other than an unfolding chaos, our ability to conceptualise events in a non-linear, non-binary manner is indispensable. The decay of large organic systems often require violent perturbation to keep life going. The parameters of signification are always up for grabs: no system is truly isolated and no individual part acts in complete autonomy such that it must descend into full entropy. To ignore the need for a sober redress toward a simplistic historic narrative is to encourage an outcome where the role of the deviant form is negated. If we ignore this challenge we can expect and deserve to live and die with the consequences.

Conclusion to the parallel narrative. Application of Research

In 2015, I was encouraged to outline a proposal for the Oslo Architecture Triennial (OAT) 2016, titled After Belonging. The impact of globalisation upon the contemporary experience of belonging is a central theme to OAT. As at least the second wealthiest nation in Europe, the architecture of Norway's capital city often expresses an impersonal, glasswork corporate style.

This is a little unfair on Oslo. Most modern cities express the same generic architecture as Oslo. However, the pedestrianised roads between apartments in the various new developments around the city centre (e.g. Tjuvholmen or Pilestredet Park), set aside for emergency access, do rather act and feel like militarised checkpoints. After a while, an intensely generic, corporate atmosphere was confirmed when a domestic drone hovered outside my seventh story window while I worked on this paper.

Commuting with the early morning business class, I can see how globalisation is part of Norway's collective psyche, both as economic frontier and cultural homeland. The triennial ambitiously also aims to thematise the issue of asylum and migration, working with the (soon to be evicted) centre for asylum seekers and refugees, the Torshov Transittmottak (TT), Oslo. Try for a moment to place yourself in the mind of a refugee. How would you react to finding yourself the subject of an architectural project called After Belonging? Ideally, with a sense of comic irony: as the British comedian Mark Steel puts it, many of the migrants arriving on our shores have somehow found enough money to make a series of precarious deals with human traffickers, escaped a war torn region, crossed treacherous oceans by any means available, scaled or otherwise outwitted the peripheral fences of continental Europe, and finally crossed into Norway, Germany or another Western European country - lazy buggers those asylum seekers!

Should Airbnb (a 'site' given equal importance in the Triennial) be discussed in the same project, the same breath as the first hand narrative of migration from the Middle East to contemporary Europe? The outcomes of the OAT will be an interesting case in point. In response to OAT, I created a project outline entitled Before Belonging.

Belonging. Being. Existence. These ideas have woven their way throughout my writing from the personal to the international and planetary scale. If we look at contemporary international migration, even if the the EU alone were to accept all 4 million refugees displaced from Syria, and one hundred per cent of them were Muslim, the percentage of Muslims in the European Union would only rise from four per cent to five per cent. Search for *The European Refugee Crisis and Syria Explained*, Kurzgesagt.

The theme of belonging brings many of today's fears together: fear of the cultural 'other', fear of ourselves, or, even a latent anxiety about who we might become in a crisis. Revealing eternal fears of death and poverty, the migration narrative of contemporary Syria, other Middle Eastern and African nations and Europe, highlights the shortcomings of the atomised, neoliberal ideology of late capitalism.

And while it is all very well throwing stones at neoliberalism I hope this paper has argued convincingly that ideological drives are, at times, so complexly intermeshed with material conditions so as to render them impotent as scape goats. As a radical, I tend to emphasis the importance of first hand knowledge and encounter with the 'other', who or whatever that might be. In the often polarised terms of migration, encounter with those who seek refuge in Europe is an inescapable part of contemporary life. Like it or not, it always has been. The real story of today's migration narrative lies ahead of us. Perhaps only in five, ten or fifteen years, will I be able to write an even remotely accurate account of what is today an unfolding challenge to many.

However, I would still like to believe that you and I can have a hand in shaping the nature of our interactions between these groups.

My proposal for the Oslo Architectural Triennial attempts to do so. As I understand the unfolding scenario, there is a critical need to communicate complex human amalgams in a clear and precise manner. The situation is complex and therefore demands a rethinking of binary perspectives. At its core, writing the application became a means of thinking though different ways of bringing unheard and marginalised narratives of inhabitation and belonging to the fore.

By recording the acoustics of different locations such as the Mosques, Churches and the bureaucratic environments often frequented by refugees and asylum seekers, this could be a way to create new knowledge around the way in which belonging, inhabitation, and privacy find resonance or dissonance in new cultural surroundings.

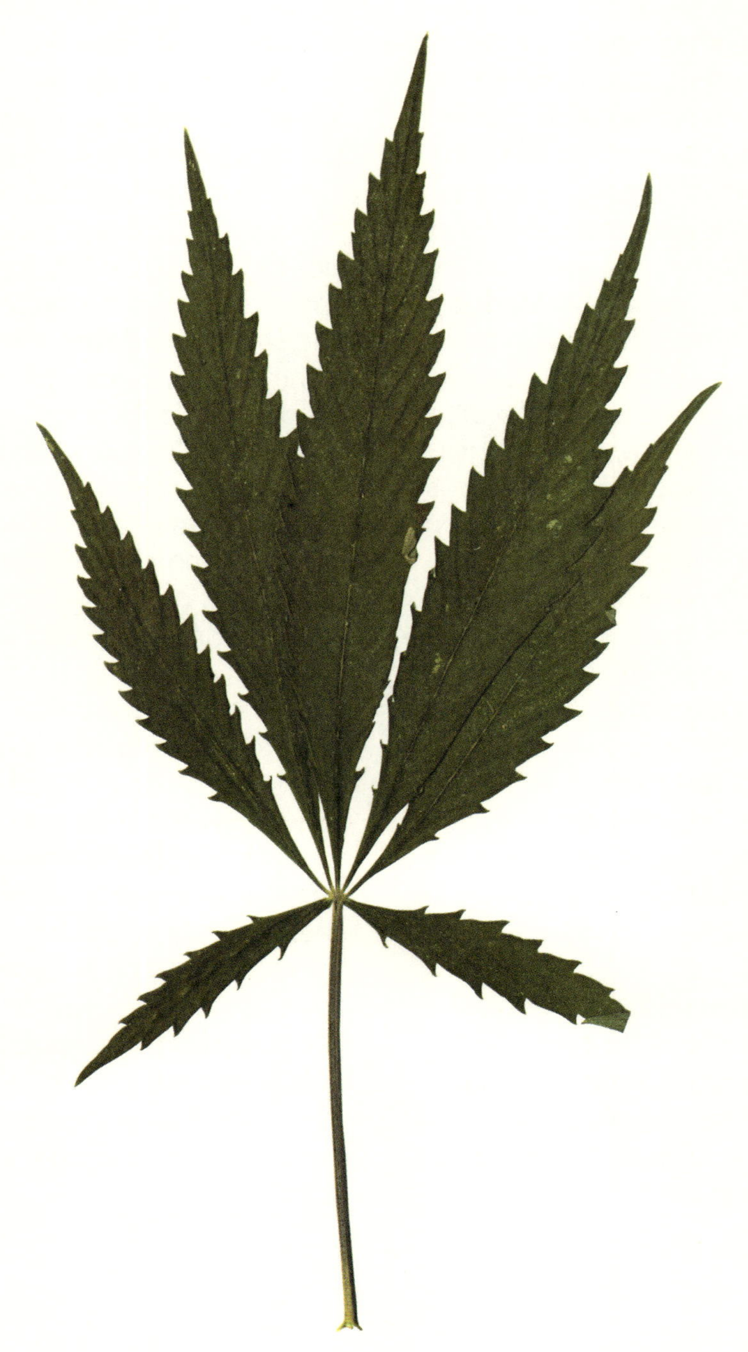

Afterword

Afterword

It is no coincidence that at the heart of this book lays a paradox about ambiguity. A tug of war exists in which ambiguity struggles against simplistic categorisation. At one end pulls freedom of expression, at the other the terror of ideological persecution. Neither force ever seems to completely engulf the other.

In my formative years I experienced multiple social and parental norms. Though they existed, I didn't seem to recognise them or else I chose to ignore many social boundaries as I grew up. In this way, a personal narrative underlies my exploration of deviancy. In hindsight, the boundaries I created for myself were equally, if not more restrictive than anything I experienced from my peers and mentors. By 2013, I recognised the perils of denying one's gender politics and decided to come out as bisexual. Performing this aspect of my identity had now become primary.

Bisexuality was radically over-emphasised within my psyche and the only option was to act it out. A paradigmatic shift gave birth to new questions, one following on the crest of another. New spaces revealed themselves amidst the ones I already knew. Depth, texture and substance: I fell in love with my city, glancing down from a studio building onto a space of permanent reinvention, the Berlin wasteland.

Foraging, graffiti, drug use and sex: a multitude of deviant behaviour converges within wastelands. They are an ideal terrain, a complimentary opposite from which to critique the formalised modern city. Deviant knowledge abides there.

It was through exploring several of these sites in collaboration with partners in the Wasteland Twinning Network, that I eventually took up a five week encampment upon an abandoned river island-wasteland in central Bulgaria. From there, I temporarily withdrew from the peopled world and began plotting the work you see before you.

So many faces accompany my memories of these events it has been impossible to make an exhaustive catalogue. My thanks go to Kathrin Wildner, Alice Creischer and Andreas Siekmann for their integrity and wisdom over the past three years of study at Weißensee Kunsthochschule, Berlin.

Thank you also to André Loebinger and team at the Bibliothek KHB for your generosity in ordering a broad range of research materials into the library. I would like to thank my father, Simon for many years of support and creative inspiration lovingly given. Thank you Matthias Einhoff, Philip Horst and Harry Sachs for your precision and enthusiasm. I would also like to thank my mother, Susan for her own boundless creativity.

Thank you, Ivar Kvaal for pointing toward the unknowable. In addition, I would like to thank Ferdiansyah Thajib for his guidance and inspiration over the past years and all the wonderful creative friends this isolated work has kept me away from, specifically Miodrag Kuč and Jan Bovelet, though there are many, many more. Shout out to the Jugend Theatrebüro and Refugee Club Impulse Berlin, who are doing great work for anti-islamaphobic, anti-racisim and migration issues and have shared so much with me.

Thank you to Lia Bergau, Jolanda Todt and Rafael Polo, for getting their hands dirty with me at the ZK/U during our time bank experiment. A big thank you to everyone at the ZK/U who has worked (and played) so hard to make it the broad and dynamic space that it is, over the past four years! My geological arguments could not have progressed without the advice of Federik Wesenlund at the Natural History Museum, Oslo.

A special thanks goes to Marcus at d.i.y Church Radio Berlin, Fergus at NTS Live, London and Syafiatudina of Radio KUNCI, Berlin/Yogyakarta: long may you broadcast freely! I would also like to thank Philipp Koller for the many hours of work that helped bring this project to completion. Thanks to Robert Heatherington for the use of The Word Made Flesh. I am incredibly grateful to Anna Kostreva who has provided strategic advice, inspiration and conceptual rigour throughout. Thanks also to Stefka Tsaneva for overseeing the printing processs of the second edition. Finally, I should like to acknowledge that without the bravery and resourcefulness of my brother William, I could never have learnt to live and work on the brutal paradise and abandoned wasteland of Adata island, Plovdiv, Bulgaria. Thanks for being there at the beginning Will!

Additional thanks to the Third Edition
As a means to continue my research outside of the printed page, in 2017 I launched sub_ɬxəɬ on 199 Radio, New River Studios London. sub_ɬxəɬ is an itinerant platform for discussion and sonic knowledge production based at ZK/U Center for Arts and Urbanistics and 199 Radio London.

I have had the enormous pleasure of working with a great many practitioners in this context. Thank you Catherine Ryan, Sybella Perry, Wassan Ali, Nina Prader, Edna Bonhomme, Joseph Dunn, Veronica Schiavo, Theatre X and Klub Al Hakawati, Nathan Gray and Snawklor. The encrypted artwork that we use throughout the sub_ɬxəɬ platform has been gratefully received from visual artist Nabil Sami.

I would also like to thank Nick Houde for his salient and timely After Trouble, above.

Thank you to Frederick Sugden at 199 Radio and to Joe Boyce for putting us in touch. I would also like to thank Nicholas Mortimer and Dj Willie One Time for their contributions to sub_ɬxəɬ radio shows. May all your skies glow like technicolored screen savers.

Postscript to the Third Edition

Postscript to the Third Edition
The first print of Here Comes Trouble arrived just weeks before the United Kingdom voted to exit the European Union. Someone asked me about Brexit at the book launch on the 16th of June, just a week before the vote, and I had to say it was possible despite the savage public murder of Labour MP Joe Cox. But who could have predicted it, really?

Then as now, no one seems to know what that political moment meant either practically or philosophically. However, it is important to note that, contrary to the class bashing that has ensued thereafter, it is now widely acknowledged that better off, protectionist middle class voters swung the vote for Brexit; to blame a racist white working class is in itself, inherently simplistic. The argument that severe cuts in public services meted out by consecutive Conservative governments triggered waves of discontent, does not suffice to explain events away. Neither, in my opinion, does the manipulation of voting behaviour through the tracking a profiling of voters online. Though, of course, both austerity and (anti-)social media played a part in amplifying xenophobia and other forms of white male exceptionalism. The greedy, redundant, British Empire assertion that two in the bush are both our god given right and in fact better than one in the hand. Funny, when you think about it, we already had a trade deal with Europe.

The second edition of Here Comes Trouble was published just weeks before the United States voted to elect an incompetent, explicitly misogynistic, racist narcissist to the United States presidency. I am beginning to regret putting out a third. Perhaps I should criticise this man more creatively, but somehow the less attention we bestow upon a petulant child as it gasps for its mothers unshackled breast the better.

Two years on and the motivation behind Here Comes Trouble to examine social, physical, economic and linguistic systems in relationship to deviancy is as pertinent as ever. Far from the comforting historization of the persecution of woman as witches and the mentally disabled as demonic, the very practice of oppressing the vulnerable and disadvantaged is, arguably, in horrific resurgence. Detention centres for newcomers and mass deportations (such as the 100 Egyptians deported from Germany on March 8th 2018 for "visa violations", as reported by The Rahnuma Daily), reflect part of a new and at the same time very old persecution of people of colour by white Europeans.

I have personally fought against historical amnesia in the production of this work. It should therefore be made clear: to equate instances of white slavery by non-European nation-states with the scale of the white transatlantic slave project - as apologists for colonial legacies do - demonstrates an unstable, racially sociopathic position.

As Paul Seabright Professor of Economics at the University of Toulouse, France, states in his 2018 BBC Radio 4 series on "Conflict and Cooperation, A History of Trade", at least twelve million slaves of colour were transported to the Americas;

(...) at its height one newly enslaved person was sent across the Atlantic every seven and a half minutes, day and night, three hundred and sixty five days a year, for one hundred years. And one person died every hour during that century as a direct product of industrial slavery carried out on the high seas, often from sickness or being thrown to drown for fear of contaminating others.

In 2018, the British government still refuses to apologise or begin restitution for these barbarous acts. If anything, Brexit expresses nostalgia for this bloody and shameful legacy while dehumanising displaced persons. Many of whom have been displaced precisely by the continued malaise of so called post-colonialism.

In 2018, one could say that since the first appearance of the book, Here Comes Trouble, the deviant form has been formulated in the oppression of the feminine. Women have moved the political discourse to a serious debate about the chronic abuses of power within patriarchy. This tuning has also caused many of us men to re-asses our past endeavours with close feeling, qualified by honest reflection. I can only hope and push for a world in which equal pay, rights and representation for men and women of all backgrounds remains among the top priorities for global power in anticipation of a better system altogether.

In this regard, the #Metoo movement is a welcome product of the new networked age. Among a bleak landscape of 'alternative facts', psychological profiling, and racially biased algorithmic policing, new tech is anything but a benevolent force today. The #Metoo movement may well be the most positive example of what the internet can achieve for progressive ideas amongst the detritus of early 21st Century digital history.

Though many dynamic, deviant forms of knowledge are the direct heirs of the new networked age, I'm also not the only one to think of the internet as a tragic form of lost commons. Outside of a serious move made by state or citizen powers to create an online environment outside of capitalist parameters, the internet is due to become a dubious ally in the construction of progressive, political debate during the anthropocene. As the nature of energy production and informational exchange mutate they give rise to new social and material paradigms.

All markets are regulated. Therefore the structures deployed to achieve this regulation, operating through technological apparatuses under predictive principles (as with thermodynamics but also internet hashtags), will require close analysis under the prism of deviant knowledge, its production and human behaviour. Humanity will always work to expand the parameters laid out by our forbears. How the novel form is received and regulated must too evolve. With new interfaces between the mechanical and the organic, that which defines the value of humanity will come under great scrutiny. The study of deviancy, therefore, does not end with the book in hand. There is, dear reader, plenty more trouble to come.

Alex Head, Spring, 2018

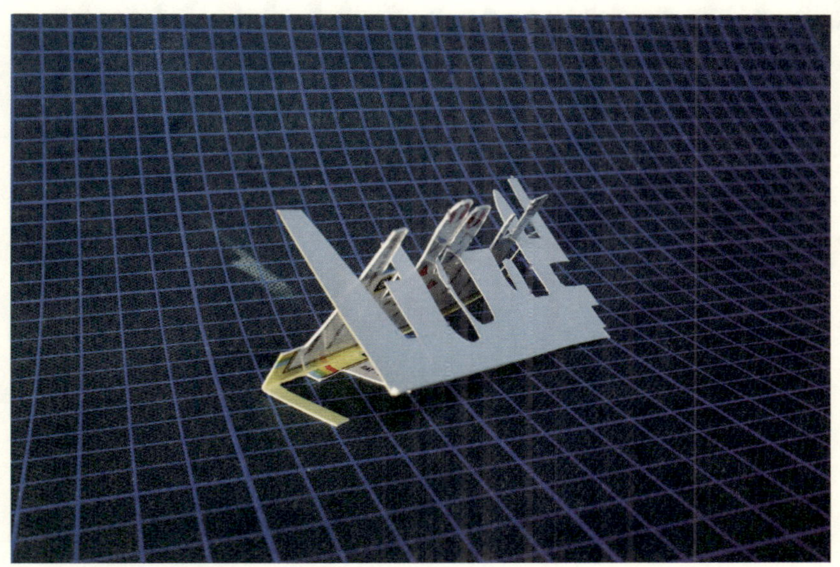

Hacked Pocket IQ Test, 2018

After Trouble

Nick Houde

After Trouble

In 2009, former Alaska governor Sarah Palin published a
memoir entitled Going Rogue: An American Story capitalizing on
a go-your-own-way narrative that would justify her political lam-
poons as merits under the bulwark of a certain American ideology
of the rebel. It was a tale of her political path to potential vice-presi-
dency alongside her "maverick" running mate; both purportedly un-
harried by the norms and mores of the political class. And they were
not alone. A grassroots movement calling itself the "Tea Party"
emerged roughly around that time in the US, subsuming an anti-Big
Government and anti-immigrant agenda within the historical ban-
ner of revolutionary defiance. Clandestine dumping of imported
tea into Boston harbor turned into patrolling the south side of the
national border on lawn chairs whilst attempting to keep their hard
earned money out of the clutches of regulation and taxation.

Laughable, contradictory, inarticulate -- they were left
to their rural enclaves of RV parks, social security benefits and a
forthright conviction that they, as citizens, had been wronged. Or so
it was then. Maybe many even see it this way today, suggesting that
these "deplorables" are the scourge against the liberal progressiv-
ism we had (apparently) all agreed on. But in truth, they were van-
guard. Not laughable but instead the prods that would usher in the
very strange and fragile geopolitical situation we in the global north
now inhabit. They were, and still are, the "anti-establishment"; the
deviants, those marginal geographically and socially.

What I mean to say by this is that the current political situation along the North Atlantic -- with its new political ecology of
populist movements now taking the helm -- are, for all intents and
purposes, a product of this deviant rhetoric. That while some of us
might sympathize with the often rural, often poor and yes -- often
ignored -- defiance of these folks, we could only do so at the pitiful
admittance that theirs is a rebellion we hope to extinguish. That is:
Here Comes Trouble has now become Here is Trouble, only this

trouble is more troublesome than we hoped, or even imagined it to be.

Surely many will disagree with me here, suggesting that the figure of the deviant is something irrevocably allied to historical accounts of admirable outcasts whose struggle and marginality point to the lamentable state of our situations, eventually undermined by influences it hoped to keep at bay. It's a deep seated idea in the European traditions afterall. Founded in Socrates and transubstantiated in the figure of Jesus; its as if the history of the West were a litany of deviant humans saving us from the tireless habituation of institutions and their governance. Agents of change; progressors of history.

While I would never deny the importance of these type of laudable acts nor the humans and the risks associated with them, it seems essential to also acknowledge the great many horrors wrought by the less savory deviants throughout history. Your fascist revolutionaries, "communist" tyrants, your seclusive-right-wing-unabomber types -- all of whom have probed the depths of human depravity. Theirs is a deviancy against the state of things from the egregious fringes of what many would see as aimless misanthropy. They are those figures we hope to extoll from our list of triumphant deviant figures, romantic and libertine. But should we -- could we -- avoid drawing equivalence? Does deviance go both ways?

It is perhaps too apt in this case to bring up the case of the lefty darling turned feudalist nightmare of a thinker Nick Land. Famed for his early work, Fanged Noumena, he himself knew just how dangerously ambivalent ideas are when left to their own devices. That once conjured, many of the best sounding ideas of democracy, freedom, Enlightenment and even rebellion live well beyond the phenomena or context they were first attributed to. They have a rather ambling, vampiric life of their own well beyond the pale of our own moral retribution and to deny this fact would be to turn a blind eye to the justificatory regimes and equivocations of the ambit of discursive regulation. Which is out and out to say that our conceptual tools are not saviours in and of themselves; they are merely tools that parasite off the lifeblood of new phenomena wanting and waiting to be written.

Land himself seems to have fallen prey to his own hyperstition as he moved from being a rather outsiderish academic philosopher to a reclusive neomedivial ethno-nationalist blogger of the NRx movement. The question remains as to how exactly that shift occurred, yet in hindsight it is easy to see how his conceptualizations of nihilism, acceleration, and a "thirst for annihilation" might very well have come to fruition in less savory formations over time. And this begs the question: did those of us influenced or vexed by his early work simply not heed his own purportments? Did we, in our haze of excitement over the creative destruction of acceleration -- of our hatred for this world as it is -- fail to see what dangers could potentially lie ahead?

Maybe. But in this regard it seems most important to think about the operation and mechanics of how these problems have been framed in the first place. At its base, that means the complications are placed in a time old political problem of whether or not the ends justify the means of any strategy for social or philosophical change. Or, better yet, how we manage and think through particular goals, shared aims, and projects as translations between generalized theoretical discourse instead of leaving concepts untethered and wandering into the ambivalence of interpretation. This is precisely the trap I think an idea of deviancy risks overlooking. Without specific and context particular aims, it lends itself as a conceptual device too malleable to be operative for any political or ethical aims. Instead, it runs dangerously close to equivocating marginal positions and beliefs -- for flattening out their topology -- that have gained their outsider status for highly divergent historical reasons. How is it afterall that we could or would discern the difference between forms of life (or thought) that are excluded from our societies (state spaces) because of their vulnerability as opposed that have been excluded through a willing and collective ethical injunction on something seen as inadmissible? There seems to be a lot of terrain between the refugee and the Nazi, despite the fact that both can and have been pushed out of normative positions and afford a moment of radical change within a liberal consensus.

Theories are powerful in that regard. The concretizations of theories in our material world shape themselves so strangely it's often difficult to trace them. Particularly when one uses metaphors across disciplines or out of context, we often fail to attend to what it is we are actually aiming at when we try to transpose the metaphor into the particularity of that which we hope to define. Philosophical and political discourses - even those in this book - are full of metaphors that provide an elegant image of organizational principles too immaterial to picture otherwise. In that way, metaphors are powerful heuristics. They are discursive technologies and as such they may be handled in very different ways, often to the dismay of those who invented them. That needs to be considered. Also, the limits of our heuristic metaphors are equally important. Taking the physical law based descriptions of physics as a metaphor, for instance, will necessarily have a rocky ride once translated into a norm based system such as culture or politics. They are, at the end of the day, fundamentally describing different types of things. Law based systems are enforced by what is physically possible, norms are enforced through the will of another (or group). Moving between these types of systems in metaphoric description, therefore, requires the careful gesture of translation that can describe and make useful how the heuristic metaphor operates in parallel and to what extent or limit point that holds true.

Norms and prescriptions in a society are tricky in that regard. Conflating them is at constant issue within idiomatic language and, more incredulously, often underlies the trenchant political projects that have come to foreclose our ability to think of another world. Mark Fisher's work on capitalist realism is a great example of this effect. Norms become "naturalized" as if they were physical laws; understood as if they were, for the most part, unchangeable, inherent, and not subject to determination by values. At the same time, norms simply as norms - as qualified aims of a group of people - can and perhaps should play a large role in advocating for a better world. I guess the trick is to state it like that; that these rules are not metaphysical, not "natural," not manifest or necessary but instead form the armature with which groups of humans (or perhaps even humanity as a whole) could find fungible ground to negotiate their values. And with that in mind, one can begin to unpack the very serious differences in a mathematical catastrophe or a change in state space from the tides of political and social upheavals driven by emboldened outsiders. And to no longer enable this conflation, makes us accountable to the very real consequences that general theories have when they are not coupled with an aim.

I feel our time is poised to deal with these question more bluntly if only we give ourselves the space and paucity of mind to reflect on ourselves. The "rogue" and the "maverick" and all their vigilante friends who have subsequently come to power have made dealing with it essential even. If we ascribe any reality to their claim for deviancy, for their own romantic ethic of marginalized outsider salvation, then we might want to reconsider this deviancy thing altogether. And by doing so, whatever we's we are, we will want to truly engage with what it is we are willing to cede from misgivings in our own political desires and mythologies. Would it be worth it to discontinue the figure of the romantic deviant in our political theology?

With rising tides between an (hopefully) emancipatory Left and an ethno-capitalist Right both positioned to dismantle the liberal consensus -- a consensus I firmly believe only actually lived in the minds of career politicians and elites -- the iron is hot once again for articulating aims for what form of deviant disruptions we are actually interested in supporting in either minor personal or large geopolitical iterations. History has shown deviancy is not enough of a concept to assure the success of any one political aim. And despite even my own subcultural proclivities, those of us on the side of emancipation ought to think about the antimony nestled between staying radically "marginal" while still advocating for general equity and inclusion in the very same social structures we hope to deny. We need a new metaphor. Afterall, doesn't being merely "against" the state of things suggest that we have no stake in getting rid of those structures once and for all? Something doesn't match up. Instead, I wonder if we could focus more on aims. Could we, for instance, try and think of what an abolition of the deviant could look like? Not in the form of excluding but of there being no possibility for such a distinction, kind of like similar claims made for prison, gender, and work abolition. What would such a social system look like? Or, to think in another direction, what would it mean for the Left to embrace the creation and negotiation of norms for more universal and emancipatory aims? After decades now of the feckless breaking down of social structures, could it be worthwhile to begin thinking about what structures might work toward these aims, whose protectionist and enabling infrastructure could only lament the incursion from some deviant undermining it?